Rise
ABOVE

Rise
ABOVE

*How one man's search for mobility
helped the world get moving*

Ralph W. Braun

The Braun Corporation®
Winamac, IN

Published by
The Braun Corporation®
PO Box 310, 627 West 11th Street
Winamac, IN 46996
www.BraunAbility.com

Publisher's Cataloguing-in-Publication Data
Braun, Ralph W.

  Rise above : how one man's search for mobility helped the world get moving / Ralph W. Braun. – 1st ed. – Winamac, IN : The Braun Corp., 2010.

  p. ; cm.

  ISBN13: 978-0-9843380-0-9

  1. Braun, Ralph W. 2. People with disabilities–United States–Biography. 3. Successful people–United States–Biography. 4. Businessmen–United States–Biography. I. Title.

HV3174.B87 B73 2010
362.40922—dc22   2009942356

Project coordination by Jenkins Group, Inc.
www.BookPublishing.com
Interior design by Yvonne Fetig Roehler

Printed in the United States of America.
20 19 18 17 16 • 8 7 6 5 4

To my parents,

for helping me up the ladder.

contents

preface   x

prologue   1

chapter one   DIRT FARMER'S SON   9

chapter two   AS HEROES GO   17

chapter three   BARRIERS AND BRIDGES   25

chapter four   THE WORLD AS A CLASSROOM   35

chapter five   MOON SHOTS   47

chapter six   ADVENTURES IN MACHINE MAKING   55

chapter seven   CHANGING TIMES   65

chapter eight   OF MENTORS AND MEN   75

chapter nine   NEITHER RAIN NOR SNOW   85

chapter ten   SPARKS FLY   93

chapter eleven   CRAZY GOOD TIMES   103

chapter twelve   MOMENT OF TRUTH   111

chapter thirteen   READY, WILLING, AND ABLE   121

chapter fourteen   PIONEER SPIRIT   129

chapter fifteen   THE FIRE   139

chapter sixteen   OUT OF THE ASHES   147

chapter seventeen   BACK TO SCHOOL   157

chapter eighteen   IT'S A SMALL WORLD   169

chapter nineteen   LET'S MAKE A DEALER   177

chapter twenty   INVENTING THE FUTURE   185

epilogue   193

acknowledgments   199

about the author   201

STILL RISING

THESE DAYS I hear the word "legacy" being tossed around a lot. It's something I think about more as I pass middle age. How will I be remembered? What will I leave behind? A legacy requires doing more than just existing through the years God gives us. It's planting a seed that grows and thrives long after we're gone.

When I reflect on Ralph W. Braun, the word legacy comes alive. The funny thing is, Ralph never aspired to build a legacy. Rather, by his will and ability, and through God's grace, it just happened. That's what makes his story remarkable. His legacy is organic, natural, without pretense, and very much alive today.

As you read his life story, you will discover the Ralph I knew—funny, smart, and a lover of life, especially the simple things. He was courageous, big hearted, creative, and ingenious. With these traits and through his circumstances came the opportunity to answer a crying need from society; the result was world-changing. His legacy wasn't born from the Tri-Wheeler or the first wheelchair lift or the first accessible vehicle. It was born from his decision to mass-produce these innovations and share them with the world.

I first met Ralph at a dinner my wife and I hosted in our home. I knew very little about him at that time. I knew that he was from Pulaski County, where I had grown up, he liked NASCAR, and he owned some kind of conversion business. That evening, Ralph wheeled out of his Entervan, and we enjoyed a three-hour dinner talking about business, politics, family, life, God, and, of course, racing. Nothing about his persona that night betrayed his incredible success.

Years later when I first visited BraunAbility's 88-acre site in Winamac, my jaw dropped. How could this be? A massive manufacturing and business complex in the heart of Pulaski County? It was so much more than "some kind of conversion business." Ralph gave me the complete tour over several hours, and at every department he'd roll up and talk with another employee, comfortably, as if they were family. I found out later that, for him, they were: his company employees were an extension of him. I was in awe of the scale of the operation and even more so at how this man engaged with his people and led with his mind and heart.

I had the privilege of spending the last seven years of Ralph's life under his leadership. As anyone who knew him well would tell you, he was fun, but he demanded respect—always challenging me and teaching. He hated meetings and bureaucracy. He loved seeing people succeed. Ralph started most conversations with, "So, what's up?" It was his way of learning whether you were on top of things. He was a magnet when our customers had the opportunity to meet him. He gave them hope, encouragement, joy, and a desire to live boldly. I can think of no stronger legacy to leave behind.

Ralph left us for eternity on February 8, 2013, but as cliché as it may sound, he's still with us. As a company, we distilled his actions, stories, and sayings into the 5 Lessons from Ralph. These lessons and his life example ensure that Ralph's legacy endures and continues to have an impact on his company, community, country, and world:

Put the Customer First—Ralph was the first customer for his products, and we now see children able to go to school, men and women able to work productively, and elderly people able to enjoy their lives through accessible transportation everywhere.

No Excuses—With so many false, man-made barriers to success for people in wheelchairs, Ralph could so easily have given up. Instead, he fought hard for accessibility and by example showed that nothing could get in the way of success if you "just put your mind to it."

Surround Yourself with Good People—Ralph valued people and understood that his success would be shared by the people he worked with and relied upon every day. He treated people fairly and with respect and fostered a mutual loyalty that was key to his success.

Never Stop Improving—Nearly 50 years of leadership came from Ralph's belief that success doesn't have a finish line. He cared about his customers and his vision for making life better for them, and he expected that same commitment from his people.

Believe in Your God-Given Ability—Ralph was asked if he would ever change anything about his life, and he unequivocally said, "I wouldn't change a thing." Ralph believed that the circumstances God gave him were meant to be for the good of others.

If you never had the opportunity to meet Ralph, you will feel like you know him once you've finished this book. And if you knew Ralph as I did, you'll enjoy returning to this book time and again to hear his words and appreciate the direct, unassuming man who never saw a barrier without also seeing a way around it. That's a legacy worth leaving.

—**NICK GUTWEIN**, President and CEO of BraunAbility

ON A hot summer day in 1947, I was told I would not live to see my 13th birthday.

I was six years old at the time and playing toy trucks and cars with my cousins Ed, Frank, Henry, Charles, and Harry outside my Aunt Elizabeth's farmhouse in Logansport, Indiana. My parents were inside, and we were in the dirt driveway. We stopped there after a visit to Riley Hospital in Indianapolis, where my parents had taken me for some medical tests.

They had noticed I couldn't do some of the things other kids my age could do. When other kids ran up stairs, I walked a step at a time and held the railing. When other kids sprang to their feet from sitting positions, I pushed myself up slowly with my hands on my knees. In a footrace of any distance,

I always fell behind. At Riley Hospital, they hoped to find an answer.

"What's wrong with you?" my cousin Henry asked. "Why were you at the hospital?"

I didn't know what to say. The doctor, a big burly guy, said I had some kind of disease that caused me not to walk and move around as well as others, but I didn't really know what it meant. At the age of six, all I knew was he gave my parents some pills and told them to make sure I took them every day. The medicine was still in the car, and I went to get it so I could show my cousins. On my way back up the driveway, the container opened, and I dropped the entire contents in the dirt.

"Help me pick these up," I said, scrambling to gather the pills and clean them off. "I don't want my parents to know I got them dirty."

"It doesn't matter," said my cousin Harry, who had just come out of the house, the screen door slamming shut behind him. "I heard our parents talking, and they said you're going to die anyway, probably before you grow up."

A thousand thoughts filled my head, and just as many feelings flooded my body. I was confused and disoriented. All at once, I wanted to curl up in a ball and cry, make a fist and punch my cousin in the mouth, and run away as far as my unsteady legs could take me. But another instinct took over: the instinct to rise above what he said to me and not let it—whatever it was—beat me. In that moment, I vowed that no matter what it took, my cousin would see me grow up.

You see, at Riley Hospital, the doctor never told me the outcome. Unbeknownst to me, he did tell my parents the following: I had muscular dystrophy, I wouldn't live past my teens, and nothing more could be done for me. He also asked my parents whether they would consider leaving me behind so the doctors could study me.

My parents were outraged. No way would they leave their child behind and have me studied like some guinea pig. They were determined to take me home and help me live in the mainstream of society.

I was ambulatory for a while, but for many years when I could no longer walk, my father carried me on his back, "piggyback" style. He was a big man, standing at 5 feet 11 inches and weighing 210 pounds. I weighed about 140 pounds, and while many fathers carry their kids around in this playful manner, it was my mode of transportation. What I didn't find out until many years later was my father had broken his back in a car accident a few years earlier. I'll never know how painful carrying me must have been because he never said a word about it.

With muscular dystrophy, muscle size and strength gradually decrease over time. Because so little was known about the disease in the 1940s, my prospects for survival seemed scant—to put it mildly.

Some in my situation would have chosen to let the government or some religious or charitable organization support them with disability payments. Others would have stayed home, with their family members acting as caretakers. Depending on the severity of their illnesses, others would have lived in institutions. Sometimes, it would have been a combination of all those methods. Any of those options would have been fine for other people, and I wouldn't begrudge them their choices, even for a moment. But theirs was not my way, and it certainly wasn't my family's way. It could have been if not for my parents' determination, for which I am eternally grateful.

I am now 69 years old. I am a father, a son, a husband, and a grandfather. I am an inventor and an entrepreneur. I am the founder and CEO of The Braun Corporation, an international company that is 48 years old and every day changes the lives of disabled customers and their families all over the world. Having survived my doctor's prognosis and outlived my cousin's prediction, I can safely join Mark Twain in saying, "Rumors of my demise have been greatly exaggerated."

I still get choked up at the memory of hearing I was going to die. At six years of age, my interest was in survival. The notion I would one day start and run a global company was beyond my wildest dreams. However, I did feel that although I had been dealt a serious challenge, I would rise above it. I also felt if I ever had the opportunity to help others rise up after being knocked down, I would do it with every last weakening muscle in my body.

However, when I started my business in 1962, it was more out of necessity than as part of a grand plan.

I could no longer walk, and although I used a wheelchair, getting around was becoming very hard. Society did not at that time know how, or care, to accommodate physically disabled people. Curbs did not have cuts in them as they do today. Ramps were not available. Cars and doorways were not built to make room for wheelchairs. Physically disabled people were treated as second-class citizens, a fact I was unwilling to accept.

That's the main reason I created the Tri-Wheeler, the world's first motorized scooter: to give me access to the life everyone else took for granted. Shortly thereafter, I also realized if I built Tri-Wheelers for others, I could give them the same gift of mobility I had and make some extra money in the process.

The odds were against me: I was a 22-year-old inventor and entrepreneur with no money and no employees and just my parents' garage as a workshop. Despite seemingly insurmountable obstacles, over the next 48 years Braun grew into a global enterprise with more than 400 dealers and 700 employees. To disabled people and their families, as well as to businesses, Braun is a well-known brand that is trusted on four continents. Thanks to the efforts of many intelligent and indispensable people, we have achieved steady and substantial growth. To this day, we are an honest-to-goodness, made-in-America, privately held company that has never moved its headquarters from the small town of Winamac, Indiana, where I was born and raised.

Our tale is far more than a recitation of our growth and global reach; it's also about how a company can be constructed around values such as compassion, competence, integrity, incessant curiosity, initiative, honesty, and good old-fashioned hard work. In many ways, Braun combines the best traits of both of my parents. The fact that a company can succeed through both empathy and empowerment is a testament to their Midwestern work ethic.

Braun has become a beloved brand to everyone who comes in contact with it. I cannot count the number of heartfelt letters we get from people who have been able to do everything from the mundane to the miraculous because of our products. Things such as attending school or going to the store, which for most people are the humdrum experiences of everyday life, become magnificent adventures for people using our vans and lifts. For someone who lived through the "dark ages" of society's attitudes toward the disabled, I cannot possibly be more satisfied over what we have wrought.

People are devoted to our brand because they experience firsthand what we are all about. Braun is more than vans with lifts: it's freedom of movement and the feeling of being empowered to go places and do things—which is why our tagline reads "Because life is a moving experience."

Because of their humility and modesty, my dad, who has passed away, and my mom, who is now 98 years old, would never accept what I am about to say: in many ways, Braun is a testament to them. For all they did for me, I am trying to do for others through the example of my life.

Writing a book was never something I thought I'd do. I thought looking back at my life and Braun's history was like trying to drive a car by staring in the rearview mirror. Now I see it differently: our best days are still ahead of us. We may be 48 years old, but like my mother, we still have a long way to go.

So why write a book now? The easy answer is the time is right. I realize this is not an adequate answer, but I believe in timing—and I'll talk about that throughout the book. Let me try to explain my reasoning for writing this book now.

First, I hope my story can encourage individuals to reach for and achieve whatever their hearts desire. My philosophy is pretty straightforward: no matter the obstacle, no matter the challenge, no matter what other people may think about you, you can rise above anything you face. Look at me. I was a poor kid from farm country. I had little formal education, I had no connections, and I was in a wheelchair when society did not accept people with disabilities. However, I was determined to be mainstream, and no one was going to stop me.

Second, I'd like to encourage struggling businesses and the country at large. The way I see it, everyone gets knocked down from time to time. In recent years, our country has been knocked flat on its back. I don't mean to minimize bad times, but tough things can and do happen. The key is what you do after you've been knocked down. You can complain and have self-pity, you can blame your circumstances on fate or some other person or entity, or you can wait for someone or something to rescue you. In my view, a business or country that takes any of those routes weakens its character. Sure, you can get help, as I did, but it's up to you to initiate your own comeback.

Third, I dream I can be an encouragement to our wounded veterans, for they are heroes to me. I have been to dozens of Veterans Affairs hospitals over the years and have countless friends and customers who are wounded veterans. They touch my heart and inspire me in my own life. Because of my muscular dystrophy, I was never able to serve alongside them, but I'd like to think that in my own way, I've been serving alongside them all these years with my products and services. Long after I'm gone, I know my company will still be serving them.

I don't expect to get rich writing this book, but I do hope to enrich others. With that in mind, a portion of every dollar from the sale of this book will go to the Ralph Braun Foundation, which is just being formed as this book goes to print. The Ralph Braun Foundation will serve as a living legacy of my work and of the efforts of our employees—past, present, and future.

Because they are inseparable, this is both my life's story and my company's story. These stories shed some light on the world of the disabled from what I think is a unique perspective, but they are not typical fodder for business schools or boardrooms, not a prescription for what people or companies should do to succeed, not how-to instructions or top-10 lists or must-dos. I present no grand management theories or magic potions that promise everlasting riches.

I offer the story of how my parents inspired me to rise above whatever life put in my way and how their example helped my colleagues and I build a company that helps others rise, too. We won some, and we lost some. We made mistakes, and we learned lessons—about ourselves and about business. Now I hope to pass all of that on through this book.

If you take one thing away from this book, I hope it's this: you can do whatever you want in life. Don't let anybody say you can't. When faced with an obstacle, never forget there's always another way. If thinking of my story helps, great—but you should always remember you can create your own story. You can rise above.

See you at the top.

chapter one

DIRT FARMER'S SON

Ability is a poor man's wealth.
-- John Wooden

M<small>Y STORY,</small> and my company's story, is like a patchwork quilt.

One piece of the quilt is how I overcame my muscular dystrophy "death sentence" to start and grow an enduring and successful business that gives people the world over the ability to lead full and active lives. Another piece is how I surrounded myself with good people, made good products, and got those products to customers who needed them. Yet another is how my colleagues and I worked our way through obstacles that kill lesser companies and in the process built something that will have lasting value long after we're gone.

Given all the challenges I've overcome, some people say my life would make a good movie. That's all well and good, but I don't need a Hollywood cast or a big production company to prove my worth.

I already have an incredible cast around me, beginning with my wife, Melody, who, in my eyes, is the most beautiful woman in the world. Behind her is a whole crew of people in supporting roles, some at our headquarters in Winamac and some in our dealerships worldwide, who have led this company to its position as the mobility industry leader.

As anyone at Braun will tell you, the real stars of my story are the people who use our products to overcome their own challenges. This story is as much about them as it is about any of us. Just like my parents demanded for me and just as I demand for myself, our customers demand to live life on their terms, to be in the mainstream of society. Where most people see walls, they see doors that have yet to be created. Where others see steps, they see ramps and lifts that have yet to be installed. Where others see chasms, they see bridges that have yet to be built. In our collective mind, we're not just making wheelchair lifts and converting vans; we're gaining the ability to get out and cast a vote, visit children and grandchildren, and go to the grocery store, just like everyone else. Our goals are not only for disabled people but also for everyone with whom we come in contact.

How is it that we think this way?

I believe Plato had it right when he said necessity is the mother of invention. As I see it, being born with a silver spoon in your mouth stifles your imagination, intuition, and initiative. It gives you a feeling of entitlement and of special privilege, as though the world owes you something just for being alive.

On the other hand, when you come from more modest beginnings, I think the opposite is true. If nothing is handed to you and you have to work for everything you get, oftentimes your imagination takes flight, you become finely attuned to your surroundings, and you have a drive that will not be denied. You feel privileged to be alive, but you also feel the world owes you nothing in return. In fact, you feel as though you have been given the ultimate gift—life—and as the good book says, "To whom much is given, much is required."

I definitely fall into the second camp because the values that formed who I am, how I live my life, and how my company does business can be traced back to my parents and grandparents.

To use an old farm expression, I come from a long line of "dirt farmers." My "official" definition of dirt farmer is someone who farms for subsistence, who does not have any hired hands, who does all of the work himself or herself. Depending on how the nickname is delivered, it can be either an insult or a compliment.

To me, it's a compliment. Lately, I've even noticed it's been romanticized in the media as being "retro-cool." The musician Levon Helm, formerly of The Band, recently wrote and recorded a song called "Poor Old Dirt Farmer." Here are some of the lyrics:

Oh the poor old dirt farmer,
he's lost all his corn,
and now where's the money
to pay off his loan?

That appropriately describes the economics of being a dirt farmer, but it does not do justice to the values and work ethic that come from working the land.

In the farm country of western Pennsylvania and Wisconsin, the path my German immigrant grandparents took before they finally set up farming in Indiana, you're as much a part of the land as the dirt you dig in. In the Midwest, "earth to earth, ashes to ashes, and dust to dust" has a very real meaning. Working hard, showing restraint, keeping your word, taking responsibility for your actions, being practical, and working as a team are sure as sunrise. Dirt farmers have the ability to delay gratification while looking to the future; they expect to reap the rewards when the timing is right and not a moment sooner. Adrenaline-fueled, temporary wins and the hottest crazes and crowds are not for them. Their survival and success come through consistency and continuous improvement. Dirt farmers are also naturally humble, primarily because they have to be: they can't control the weather and therefore can't change many of their circumstances. However, while dirt farmers can't say when there will be floods, freezes, or fires, they can tend to their machinery, livestock, and supplies. In other words, they can accept the things they cannot change and take charge of the things they can.

That description fits my grandfather, Frances (Frank) Braun. Grandpa Braun, on my father's side, born in 1860, was the youngest of nine children from the small community of Lohn-weiler, Germany. He came to America with the rest of his family in 1875. Most of the family settled in Wisconsin, but my grand-father made his home near Winamac, Indiana. That's where my own father, Joseph, was born in 1908.

They lived a hardscrabble existence.

While a lot of Depression-era farmers headed west for what they thought would be the greener pastures of California, my grandfather stayed put. He lived in a little trailer house on land that I, incidentally, would buy and build a home on for my own family in 1974. Right or wrong, he simply would not give in. He was stubborn and too proud to be told what to do. Dedicated to his family and community, he wouldn't dream of uprooting them or leaving their side to go find work. Although he was not alone in the way he thought and acted and he was not one to readily share his innermost thoughts, I do know how he felt, especially on the issue of community.

As was often the case, when Depression-era dirt farmers lost their homes and lands to creditors and were sent, heartbroken, into poverty, most people in the community pulled together to help one another out. However, some chose money over community and had no problem profiting off those less fortunate. These people cared more about their own lives than the lives of their neighbors.

This kind of behavior and attitude did not sit well with my grandfather. Helping your fellow man was something in which he strongly believed, and he passed it on to my father and my father on to me. I can't say I'm perfect at being a servant to humanity, but I always try to do my best.

It was not uncommon in those hard times for "country folk" to eat rabbits, raccoons, squirrels, woodchucks, and pretty much anything else that could be shot or caught in a trap. My grandparents were getting by with a little more success and were able to take care of themselves somewhat better than other people in similar situations. As in most dirt-farming families, the roles were clear: my grandfather worked hard to put food on the table, and my grandmother cooked it. You might imagine from this division of labor that perhaps my grandfather was hard and my grandmother soft, but that's not true. My grandfather may have butchered a hog and brought it into the house, but my grandmother had to prepare, salt, and cook it. Although my grandfather might have been physically tough, my grandmother was both physically and emotionally tough.

My grandfather wore a beat-up hat, a blue work shirt, a vest, jeans, and constantly mended shoes. He was a hardworking, down-to-earth farmer who spent his days working the land and getting his hands dirty. My grandmother wore a faded flower-print dress and old shoes that she also frequently mended. She had one other dress, a gray Mother Hubbard, with a rounded neckline and a flowing skirt that scared their horse when the fabric blew in the breeze. Together, they were very modest and were not so much concerned about their clothing as they were about feeding their family and doing their chores.

Other men might have worn their jeans rolled up at the ankles, with cowboy boots, a Stetson hat, a plaid shirt with pens in the shirt pocket, and a belt with a huge buckle, like James Dean or Steve McQueen—who, by the way, were born in Marion and Beech Grove, Indiana, respectively. Men like that were rugged and coarse and wanted the world to know it. Those people were not as connected to the land as my grandparents were. Others used any extra money they earned to grab the attention of the opposite sex. If my grandparents earned any extra money, my grandfather might buy new overalls and my grandmother a new dress, but they would have put most of the money back into the farm. They thought of clothing in practical terms; style was not part of their concern. The garments on their backs were just a means of modestly covering their bodies and protecting them from the harsh and unforgiving Indiana weather.

On my mother's side of the family, my great-grandfather was a tailor by profession, and fabric and clothing obviously played a more substantial role in his life. His name was William Friske. He was born in Germany in 1868, and his family moved to Indiana in 1879.

Although my great-grandfather's son, my Grandpa Asa Freeman, became an Indiana dirt farmer just like those on the Braun side of my family, my great-grandfather's skills as a tailor would be passed down to my mother and then down to me. As a consequence, both my mother and I used our tailoring abilities as a means to get various things we wanted. For example, my mother, one of 12 children, was the only member of her family to go to college. She paid for her education by tailoring other families' clothes and working as a nanny for a lawyer who had a large family. Later, when I made my first scooters, my mother sewed the fabric on the seat cushions.

My mother also taught me how to "peg" pants, which was something I did as a teenager to earn extra money. In the 1950s, pegged pants were the style of the day, and I used to my advantage the desire of young men to be cool with their peers and with the girls. I would take a pair of Levi's, and, using my mother's sewing machine, I would taper the pants so close that a guy could barely scrunch them on over his feet. It was a big deal because he could show his ankle and a little of his leg—and prove that he was somebody because he could afford to pay someone to peg his pants. I was that someone.

Besides benefiting from the hereditary traits of hard work, solid values, and care for fellow people that were passed on to me by my ancestors, I also learned, by osmosis, much more. At an early age, I learned how to be in the right place at the right time, to make the most of an opportunity, and to trust my instincts—all of which would be recurring themes throughout my life.

My dirt farmer forebears may not have had much money, but what they gave me was far more valuable than mere dollars and cents. They gave me the drive to make the most of my ability and the compassion to help others make the most of theirs.

Their timeless gifts helped me create my company, and for that, I am blessed beyond compare.

chapter two

AS HEROES GO

*What lies behind us and what lies before us are
tiny matters compared to what lies within us.*

‑‑ Ralph Waldo Emerson

WHEN SOMEONE asked me recently
who my heroes were as a child, the question stopped
me in my tracks. No, that's understating it. I believe
I turned my head, groaned, and excused myself to
leave the room so I could attend a "meeting" I had
suddenly "remembered."

Why did I respond like this to such an innocent
question? Do I have no heroes? Like anyone growing
up in the 1940s and 1950s, I certainly had plenty
of heroic figures to choose from: Generals Dwight
David Eisenhower, George S. Patton, and Douglas
MacArthur; Presidents Franklin Delano Roosevelt
and Harry S. Truman; and scientists Dr. Jonas Salk,
inventor of the polio vaccine, and Albert Einstein,
who won the Nobel Prize for his work in theoretical
physics, were just a few.

Do I not think military veterans are heroes? During my childhood, soldiers fought wars in Europe, Japan, and Korea. When I was a young adult, they fought in Vietnam. They gave their lives and limbs so others could be free, so citizens in this country and abroad could retain their way of life, and so children and grandchildren everywhere could one day have a chance at leaving this world a better place than when they entered it.

Yes, I do believe in heroes, and those I've mentioned are some of the greatest. The world has seen and will see many more heroes, from all walks of life. So why was I uncomfortable being asked for examples of my childhood heroes?

I wince when saying this, but perhaps it's because of all the times I've been called a hero myself.

This will come as no surprise to everyone who knows me and, most of all, to my family, friends, and colleagues, but I am by no means a hero. In fact, I know that by even denying that I am one, I risk the admonishment of my 98-year-old mother, who to this day still has no problem keeping things in perspective for me. Better yet, to use one of her phrases, she has no problem letting me know when I'm getting "too big for my britches."

You see, I don't mind being admired or looked up to because of who I am as a person or because I have built a successful business. What I do mind is being called a hero for doing virtually the same things as everyone else. I'm not the only one; I know plenty of other people with disabilities who feel the same way.

Fortunately, my parents helped me understand and prepare for this complicated dynamic, both in their words and by the example of their actions. As I said earlier, they demanded that I be in the mainstream of society and did everything possible to make it so. They said I was the same as everyone else and just as people without disabilities didn't walk around marveling at how they weren't disabled, I shouldn't go through life bemoaning the fact that I was. Instead, I should work hard, keep my word, be faithful, and practice all the other values their own parents taught them.

As for hard times and heroes, I like the words of Alabama Governor Bob Riley, who also comes from a long line of farmers: "Hard times don't create heroes. It is during the hard times when the 'hero' within us is revealed."

That describes my parents in a nutshell. Though neither one of them would want me to "brag on them," the story of their character and circumstances gives a far clearer understanding of me, as well as of my company.

In 1930, while my dad was in his early twenties and still wooing my mom from his home in Winamac, he had stopped dirt farming and gotten work as a custodian on the night shift at Holy Name Hospital in LaPorte, Indiana. My mother was attending the Indiana Business College in South Bend, working as a house cleaner, and mending clothes, just like her grandfather did. They were both hardworking, enterprising people, to say the least.

One August evening, as my father was driving his girlfriend and future bride, Olive Freeman, through Knox, Indiana, on her way back to school in South Bend, a driver crossed the center line and struck them head-on. An ambulance took my father to LaPorte, to the very hospital he worked for. Though I have no knowledge of this, it would not surprise me in the least if he had the ambulance take him to LaPorte just so he could be there for work the next day.

When he got to the hospital, the doctors examined him and found he had suffered a compound fracture to his right leg and extensive internal injuries; to make matters worse, he had broken his back so badly they had little hope for him. My mother miraculously escaped any serious injury, apparently because she was thrown from the vehicle. They thought my father would not make it to the next day, so they put him on a gurney and left him in a hallway. It is almost unimaginable to me that they would be so callous and uncaring with another person's life, but that's what they did.

As my dad lay in agony in the dimly lit hallway for hours, forgotten about and left to die, a miracle of true heroism occurred. Winamac doctor Thomas Carneal, who had sent a patient to the LaPorte Holy Name Hospital to receive some specialized care, happened to walk down that hallway at that very moment to visit his patient. As he passed my dad, the doctor looked up briefly from the chart he was reading and glanced at him. In a double take right out of the movies, he went back to the gurney, leaned over, and took a closer look. "Why, I'll be. Joe Braun, what are you doing lying in this hallway?"

As my dad tried to mumble out an answer, the doctor took charge and barked orders to those around him. In almost no time, an operating room was reserved, a team was assembled, and the doctor went to work surgically saving my dad's life.

Now that's what I call a heroic act.

It's funny how life's circumstances bring people together. Dr. Carneal had first opened a private hospital in Winamac in 1920. Staffed with four nurses and eight beds, the hospital met the needs of Winamac residents until 1948, when Dr. Carneal began sending patients to out-of-county hospitals to receive more advanced care than he could provide at his local hospital. Although he closed his private hospital—the last of its kind in Indiana—he was not done yet. He had a bigger vision: the construction of a larger, more modern hospital that could serve all of Pulaski County. Upon completion of Pulaski Memorial Hospital, Dr. Carneal became chief of staff. Eventually, all five of my children would be born in that hospital, and my employees would receive their health care there as well.

As for my father, after the operation, he obviously couldn't continue his job as a custodian, so he moved in with his older sister on a small farm back in Winamac. As he went through rehabilitation and his back grew stronger, he continued to court my mom. This was a man who would not be kept down—and neither would my mom, who was self-financing her education by working several jobs.

Finally, though my dad had recovered enough strength to return to work, instead of going back to his custodial job at the hospital, he went to something he knew—farming—only this time he would farm on land he didn't own. He became a tenant farmer, which some might say was a step below dirt farmer because he was digging in someone else's dirt and not his own. What's more, he did this even after breaking his back. Although he had healed, his back was not what it was before the accident and would bother him for the rest of his life. Years later, when he and I would work together on something, I'd sometimes see the pain etched on his face, so I knew it bothered him. I never said anything about it, and neither did he; he just went on with life.

Now, I don't want to give the impression I think people should hide their feelings or deny their pain. After all, terrible things sometimes happen in life, and people hurt very deeply. How they choose to deal with the pain is entirely up to them. In my father's case, if asked about it, he'd answer, but he wouldn't dwell on it, and he wouldn't proactively start talking about it. Rather, he looked at his bad back as an obstacle that needed to be overcome, not as an excuse that could be used to justify a diminished life.

That lesson has meant everything in my life and has stuck with me in more ways than I can count. The thing is my father never had to undertake a fancy "communications campaign" to get this point across to me. He never wrote a book to "codify" his "theories." He did not hang posters on the walls of our house or create laminated wallet cards to be used as constant reminders of how he felt about things. He did not gather our family in the living room twice a year and give us a speech about his goals for the year or how he expected us to live our lives. He taught us by example, and we knew what to do.

That's kind of how I do things at my company. For instance, almost every day when I arrive at work, I go straight to the shop floor to talk with our engineers and production workers. I don't do it because some management textbook or high-priced consulting guru told me "management by walking around" improves "employee morale" and "has a direct correlation with productivity gains." I don't do it so I can "take the temperature of my employee base" so I can "engage them in a meaningful way" and thereby "ensure their loyalty and dedication."

Give me a break.

Over the years, many well-meaning consultants have actually tried to convince me to give them a lot of money so they could tell me these things. Now, we're not a billion-dollar company—though I can see that in our future—and maybe when we get bigger, we'll have to worry about such nonsense, but today our employees know exactly what to expect from me, and I like that.

So why do I go down to the shop first thing every morning? The truth is I love it. I absolutely love it. I love seeing guys with grease on their hands, cutting metal and piecing it together to create something that wasn't there before. I love looking inside a van with a group of engineers so we can figure out our way around a problem, such as giving passengers more room for their chairs, installing a little cubbyhole to store their things in, or making the sliding door fit more snugly. I love the smell of metal being cut and the noise of banging hammers, revving engines, and high-tech lasers. Most of all, I love the ideas that flow out of the place. Every single day, the people of my company are coming up with ideas that will improve the lives of an awful lot of people. This gives me great satisfaction, but to be honest, I do it mostly because I love it.

That brings me back to my parents, who told me to find something to do that I loved and then do it with all my heart. Actually, that's probably a little too touchy-feely for what they really said. It was probably more like, "Boy, you better do what you love 'cause once you start working, you're going to be at it for a long time."

After my father recovered from his injury, farming was something he was familiar with, so that's what he turned to. He also married my mom, a beautiful, talented, and intelligent woman. Together, they moved twice in rapid succession, as my dad took on work as a tenant farmer. They also had their first child, my sister, Joan.

Three years later, a few months after I was born on December 18, 1940, my parents came upon a unique opportunity. They moved our family to a 60-acre farm and evergreen nursery in Winamac, where my dad took on a job as a horticulturist and tenant farmer. The nursery was owned by I. J. Matthews, who sold the evergreens in his retail store in Gary, Indiana.

He would call my dad from the store in Gary and say he was sending a truck down to Winamac to pick up 15 trees the next day. My dad would dig up all of those trees and prepare them for the truck, bad back and all, no questions asked. At the end of the day, as my mom tried to nurse him through the night and ease all the discomfort, he was in so much pain it was almost as if he'd been in the accident all over again. Yet he never complained. He did this job for 10 years, and though I can't say he loved his work, he didn't dislike it.

My dad worked hard for everything he got, which wasn't much. More than anything, he loved his family and was content to take care of us. That's why, about six years into his experience at the tree nursery, he and my mom took me to that hospital in Indianapolis that fateful day to see whether they could improve my life. That's why when the doctor told my parents it would be a good idea for them to leave me at the hospital so they could study me, they said no. That's why my dad carried me on his damaged back, my mom tried everything conceivable to find solutions to my problems, and, together, they showed me the way to a life well lived.

As heroes go, I'd have to put my mom and dad at the top of the list.

chapter three

BARRIERS AND BRIDGES

We fight, get beat, rise, and fight again.
-- General Nathaneal Greene

INDIANAPOLIS IS home to one of the most famous speedways in the world. Though I can't say for sure how fast my father and mother were driving on the day we left Riley Hospital in Indianapolis with my diagnosis of muscular dystrophy, I can be certain of one thing: their thoughts were racing.

To begin with, they had a nine-year-old daughter to take care of, my sister, Joan. Faced with my dire prognosis, they must have wondered how they were going to take care of both of us at the same time. Things didn't look good for me, and based on what they'd been told, I would require more and more care as time went on. The last thing they wanted to do was show preferential treatment to one child over another. Even if Joan was mature and understanding for her age—which she was—she was still going to get the short end of the stick sometimes. That was just an unfortunate consequence of the reality my parents were faced with. However, I do know they always tried their hardest to make things equal for us.

My father also had his own bad back to worry about. As my condition got worse, he knew more would be required of him from a physical standpoint. That had never stopped him before, and it wouldn't this time, but he did have to think about it, not just in moving me around but also in figuring out how he could alter our physical environment to accommodate me. Would a wheelchair be needed? Special ramps? Room modifications? A new car? At the time, my parents thought I wouldn't even make it to the age of 13. They had to wonder how fast all of this was going to happen and how much time they had to prepare.

Another obstacle was society's attitude toward the disabled, which, at the time, was not exactly enlightened. Even President Franklin Delano Roosevelt, who could have served as a role model for people with disabilities, missed the opportunity by keeping the fact he was in a wheelchair a secret for 24 years after he was diagnosed with polio. Closer to home, you did not often see people with disabilities, physical or otherwise, out in public. With that as a backdrop, my parents had to wonder: Would kids give me a hard time at school? Would my friends treat me any differently? Would the school administration make the necessary adjustments so I could get the same education as everybody else?

As tenant farmers, they also had to be concerned, not because of their choice of profession but because it produced very little money. Surely, taking care of me would cost a lot of money, but where was it going to come from?

Finally, doctors were another issue. My parents had nothing against the medical profession, but the doctors in Indianapolis gave them no help or hope. Naturally, my mom and dad had to wonder whether something else could be done.

They looked for that something else nearly 500 miles west, in Clear Lake, Iowa.

My mom and dad had heard about a radio wave clinic in Clear Lake that was doing cutting-edge work with patients who were in poor physical shape, and they wanted to see whether the clinic could do anything for me. Today, people see alternative medicine as a common, complementary form of treatment—for example, in Perth, Australia, the Radiowave Therapy Clinic is devoted to treating cancer patients with radio waves—but in 1946, radio wave therapy was way ahead of its time. According to critics of the practice, it still is.

Despite the expense, my parents would not be deterred. They scraped money together, put us into the family car, and drove to Clear Lake. With the big interstate highways we now have, today that trip would take about eight hours, but in those days, it was quite a journey. About halfway to Clear Lake, we spent the night with some relatives. The next morning we continued the trip, and some of those relatives came with us.

I can recall the experience like it was yesterday.

We got inside the building, and the place was filled with people seeking help with asthma, polio, cancer—you name it. It was packed in there, like a big-city emergency room on a Saturday night.

A woman took me into an inner room with a big box in the middle that was about 10 inches wide, a foot high, and 4 feet long, with protruding electrical tubes that were 8 inches high and 4 inches in diameter. Four metal kitchen chairs were backed up to the box and encircled it. The stations were marked 1, 2, 3, and 4. She told me to sit at station 1, where I was joined by three others. Then she went behind us, adjusted some dials on the box by using a special instrument, and left the room. We sat there for 30 minutes, until she came back in and told us to move to station 2. Once there, she again went behind us, adjusted the box, and left the room. We repeated this process for the rest of the stations.

I had no idea what was being done, and it seemed like it was going on forever. I wasn't really scared because I didn't feel anything and I knew my parents were nearby, but it was definitely odd and intriguing at the same time. I mean, who experienced anything like that in 1946? Being bombarded with radio waves, all set to different frequencies, for long stretches of time? Day after day, for each visit? This was something H. G. Wells might have dreamed up.

For subsequent visits, my mother took me out of school, and we traveled together on the train, through Chicago and all the way to Clear Lake. Just the train ride alone was fascinating for a wide-eyed young motorheaded kid like me. I loved the sound of the whistle, the clanging of metal, and the chug-chugging of the train as it lurched to a start and then hurtled its way down the tracks.

Once in Clear Lake, we stayed with people whose homes were close by the clinic. Every day, we'd go across the street so I could get my treatments. We continued these treatments up until the time it became terribly difficult for me to walk and then ceased to go any longer.

It cost my parents every cent they had. If you ask my mother, it was invaluable; she believes it saved my life.

She doesn't care that we later found out—just a few years ago, by a blood test—that I do not have Duchenne, the fatal form of muscular dystrophy that would have indeed killed me by the age of 13. All she knows is I survived past the time the doctor said I would die. What's more, I never got colds, measles, chicken pox, or any of the things my sister had, despite being in close contact with her at the house when she was infected with all of those illnesses. My mother says that alone was worth it.

Anyway, how could I argue with my 98-year-old mother? If she thinks radio wave treatments were my salvation, so be it. I love her for everything she's ever done for me, those treatments included.

There's an interesting side story about Clear Lake that also says something about how our family lived our lives. About 15 years ago, after my father passed away, we flew my mother and a few of her friends to visit the historic stone Grotto of the Redemption in West Bend, Iowa, which is near Clear Lake. My mother and I used to pass it in the days we traveled out there by train.

The grotto appealed to us for several reasons. We were a devout Catholic family who went to church every Sunday and on holy days and abided by the Ten Commandments. For example, my cousin Virginia, who is now 85 years old and was one of my Aunt Elizabeth's daughters, became a nun. For another thing, I spent the first nine years of my schooling getting a Catholic education, which provided me with solid teaching and moral values that have stayed with me my whole life. In times of turmoil and desperation, I've always known my faith is available to me. Finally, the grotto was close by where the radio wave clinic used to be, and we wanted to visit the spot where I got my treatments so many years ago. Unfortunately, the building that housed the clinic was no longer there, but the grotto was, and my mother and I enjoyed our visit immensely.

For those unfamiliar with the Grotto of the Redemption, it was the lifelong work of Father Paul Matthias Dobberstein, a German immigrant born in 1872. As a young seminarian, Father Dobberstein, who had pneumonia and was close to death, prayed to the Virgin Mary to save his life. As a token of his faith, he pledged to honor her with a shrine if he lived. He survived, began building the grotto in 1912, and continued working on it until the day he died, in 1954. His idea was to provide the grotto for all who came seeking inspiration, spiritual renewal, and a strengthening of their faith. As Father Dobberstein once said, "If your messages are carved in stone, they are well nigh imperishable."

That trip was illuminating for several reasons but for one in particular: it was a reminder that my parents and the messages they gave me were solid as a rock.

In the Winamac of 1950, our lives were about to take a pivotal turn.

In the 10 years after I was born, the average cost of a house had gone from $3,920 to $8,450, the price of a gallon of gas from 11 to 18 cents, and the cost of a new car from $850 to $1,500. The average annual income had also improved, from $1,725 to $3,210, but our family was making far less than that. On a global basis, following the end of World War II, the economies of the Western world boomed, which led to the start of a consumer-fueled economy that seemed to have no bounds.

On the home front, my parents began looking for a better opportunity.

As a tenant farmer, my dad didn't feel like he was making the most of his talents or that he was being challenged enough. His age was advancing, and his health was not what he wanted it to be. He had been saving his money over the years, the broader economy was picking up, and he had grown tired of working for someone else's future instead of his own. The time was right for him to buy his own farm.

I remember going with my mom and dad to look at prospective farms when I was only nine years old. We went from farm to farm, and although they knew coming up with the money to buy one would be difficult, nothing we saw seemed to satisfy them. They talked it over and finally came to the realization they weren't really going to be making much of a change by buying a farm. They could own a farm, but they would still be farmers.

They had nothing against farmers—that's how they had been making a living—but my dad wanted to stretch beyond what he'd been doing. In addition, my mom felt like she was also not making the most of her talents. With her college education, which was pretty hard to come by in those days, neither of them could envision her bouncing through the fields on a tractor.

Then they discovered an opportunity that would enable them to retain their association with the farming community. It would fully utilize the combined skills of both my father and my mother because to get it, they had to come as part of a packaged deal.

Instead of buying a farm, they bought a 1,000-gallon Marathon Oil and Gas truck and became a bulk distributor. They had what was called a bulk plant, consisting of several large gas, oil, and diesel tanks. My father would fill up his truck, drive it around to farmers and homeowners, and then sell them the fuel and replenish as needed.

What role did my mother play in this operation? Marathon required the person getting the distributorship to have accounting and bookkeeping experience, and my mother had that in abundance. As a teenage boy growing up in the Depression, my father had dropped out of school in the eighth grade to earn money for the family, which was common for many boys. Consequently, he did not have the kind of education needed to fulfill Marathon's bookkeeping requirements. Combined with my father's people skills, work ethic, and initiative, my mother's financial ability sealed the deal.

It was then that we moved off the farm and into a house in town. The backyard had a garage for my father to keep his truck in. Twelve years later, long before Apple Computer started on its path to success in Steve Jobs's parents' garage, my father put the truck outside, and that garage became my company's first building.

As a people person who spent his days with customers, my dad did a lot of listening. He had an intuitive sense of when he needed to talk and when he needed to listen. I can remember him talking with customers on the phone at home, and the only thing you'd hear on his end was, "Yes," "No," "Is that so?" "Well, what do you think?" and so on. Then, the person on the other end would thank him for his "advice," and he would move on to the next call. He was in his element: he enjoyed his work, and he was very good at it. He and my mother, they made a great team, both at work and in life.

One of my father's philosophies was that life is a ladder that you always want to be climbing—up. He said if you're not climbing up, you're not going anywhere. You've got to remember that for every rung you climb, some folks probably have a hold on your pant leg and are trying to bring you down. Consequently, you've got to be able to shake them loose, get to the next rung, and keep climbing. Never, ever sink to their level.

One of the ways you keep climbing up, he said, is to always surround yourself with good people who aren't going to try to pull you down. You want people you can trust instead of people who engage in backbiting and petty gossip. You want people who are flexible, who will challenge you, and who are not afraid to fail instead of people who are dishonest, greedy, or cling to power. Whether you've known them for a week or 25 years, if they exhibit the qualities that will pull you down, you have to shake them off.

There's another equally important aspect of his ladder philosophy, one I've tried to pass along to my own children: when people are helping you climb and not hindering your progress, it's also your responsibility to help them.

This is part of what I love about my business. As I've been able to have a life of mobility, I've also been able to help others have the same. Bearing witness to people's gratitude for the help you've given them is priceless.

My dad also adhered to a flip side of his philosophy. When Wisconsin Senator Joseph McCarthy was on his famous Communist witch hunt in the 1950s, attempting to drag people through the mud and ruin their lives and reputations, President Dwight Eisenhower was asked to comment on what was being called "McCarthyism." His response was short and sweet—or pungent, depending on how you look at it: "Never get into a pissing match with a skunk."

My father liked this homespun wisdom and employed it often. His philosophy was that if you were faced with something negative in life that could smell you up when you could just as easily walk away, you should choose to be nonconfrontational and walk away.

At the same time, my father never backed down from a fight he thought was worthy of his effort. He won some, and he lost some, but when it came to the issue of whether I would be in the mainstream of society, he kept swinging.

One of those fights was with the local school board, which had no interest in making sure I got an education yet was determined to teach my dad a lesson.

chapter four

THE WORLD AS A CLASSROOM

Getting results through people is a skill that cannot be learned in a classroom.

-- J. Paul Getty

ONE OF the things I'm most proud of at Braun is the amount of learning and conversation that takes place with and on behalf of our customers.

I'm sure some of it is similar to behavior you'll find in many companies, such as when we study lean manufacturing principles and discuss how we can apply them to our products and processes. On any given day, a walk through the halls of our company will reveal conference rooms filled with people discussing how they can save steps in the manufacturing process, take the best of one method and apply it to another, and so on. In these rooms, people are writing on whiteboards, asking questions, and arguing for one way over another. It is a beehive of activity with one goal in mind: producing products that will help our customers live their lives.

Another way we learn is through our customer service representatives. These are not people sitting in some country a couple of continents away and reading from scripts as they attempt to answer questions—far from it. Our people, like our manufacturing employees, are sitting in Winamac, a short distance from any engineer or production worker, where they can ask their questions and get answers in real time. Part of this is because of the special relationship our customers have with our products and people, some of whom are disabled themselves.

For example, Burnie Blackmon, who first came to work for us in 1973, broke his neck in a diving accident when he was a teenager. Burnie bought his first motorized scooter from us, as well as a van with a lift. Just a few months later, he became an employee and set up my first real accounting system. Eventually, he was hired full time and worked with me in sales. He still works for us and deals with customers day to day. People can relate to Burnie, and he can relate to them. Like all of our customer service people, that comes from listening intently, building relationships, and not trying to force-fit solutions. As a result of this approach, our customers make us better, and they make our products better as well. Because they tell us what they're dealing with and how our products could be modified to meet their needs, they act as cocreators who think along with us instead of waiting for the next product release.

Perhaps the biggest amount of learning takes place in our dealerships, where salespeople and customers interact in an even more personal way. Nothing can replace the feedback we get from salespeople about why some things work or how they could work even better. Moreover, nothing can replace the energy and satisfaction we get when we hear a salesperson relay how we made a difference in someone's life. There's a video on the BraunAbility Web site that powerfully illustrates this concept.

The video begins with Samantha Bartlett laughing and riding in a go-kart with her father. You hear her parents saying how it's good to see her laugh and smile and have a good time. When you see her in this way, you can tell that she's just like any other little girl—that is, until you hear her parents start talking about the accident that changed their lives.

In December of 2001, Samantha and her mother were driving across a bridge when another driver lost control of her vehicle and careened toward the Bartletts' car. With no room to maneuver, the two cars collided, resulting in both being totaled. Samantha was instantly paralyzed from the waist down and taken to the hospital, where she spent the next 48 days.

Over the next few years, Samantha's parents tried to make a used four-door Buick Regal work as their family's transportation. However, with Samantha in an upper-body brace and no room for her wheelchair, it was very difficult to get her in and out of the car without making her extremely uncomfortable. The process was tiring and emotionally draining for everyone, but, like my family, the Bartletts were not a family that shrank from challenges either.

For years, as Samantha's father drove to work, he passed the Superior Van and Mobility dealership in Indianapolis, Indiana, and thought about getting one of our lift- or ramp-enabled vans. He thought about how much easier his family's life would be if they had a vehicle that could accommodate their needs. He didn't say it, but I can imagine he wondered whether his daughter felt like she was a burden to the family. He knew she wasn't, and he would not, under any circumstances, want her ever to feel that way.

As someone who has spent most of his life in a wheelchair, I know what it's like to feel as if you're a burden, even if no one else thinks you are. It's awful.

In any case, Samantha's father started looking into what it would take to get one of our vehicles. He had his mind set on an Entervan and brought Samantha to the Superior dealership to look at it. That's when she met Matt Ritter, who was both a superior salesman and a Superior salesman.

Matt was also in a wheelchair as a result of an accident, so right away he and Samantha had something in common. When they began talking, there was an instant connection. Because he was also in a chair, he was able to personally show her how to get in and out of the van and talk with her about how he experienced the van. He talked with her as a peer, because Matt recognized that she truly matters. That's where the magic happens, between salesperson and customer. Braun may be the instrument that brings people together, but it's the sharing of life in full bloom, such as the conversation between Matt and Samantha, that makes the world turn.

As Samantha's father said in the video, life for Samantha and the rest of the family would be considerably different without the van; they'd be lost without it. Her mother even went so far as to call it a godsend because Samantha finally seemed "just as normal as you and me."

That normalcy, that idea that Samantha could be in the main-stream of society, is exactly what my own dad had expected for me. Like Samantha's father, he would routinely drive by build-ings that were otherwise inaccessible and think of what could be possible if people would open not only the doors but also their minds.

One of those buildings was the public school I was supposed to attend in Winamac. When my father started asking questions about what could be done to help me have the same experience as other students, he was sent to the principal's office—in more ways than one.

A new school was being built in Winamac. Most people in town were happy to have such a nice new building in which to educate their children, but for our family, there was one big disappointment: the new school would be inaccessible.

Although the old school was three stories, I'd arranged my class schedule to include only courses offered on the ground floor. I still had several classes to complete; I just couldn't get to them because they weren't on the first floor.

I'd need an elevator to get to my classes, so my father went to the administration and made a sensible case that one should be installed in the new school. He reasoned that I—and any other student with a disability—deserved access to both levels of the school like everyone else.

They said no, a response they'd regret 20 years later when they finally did install an elevator, probably at 10 times the expense they would have incurred if they'd listened to my dad.

Why would they make such a shortsighted decision? In those days, most of society believed that educating a disabled person had no real benefit. I wasn't going to amount to anything anyway, so why bother?

Of course, that only spurred my father on. The more he talked, the less they listened. Finally, they came up with a compromise: they would install a phone in the second-floor classrooms so I could listen in on what was happening.

I've heard of "distance learning," but that's quite a stretch.

My father thought it was a ridiculous idea and once more said he would do everything in his power to help me be as normal as everyone else. We refused the telephone option.

In response, the school administration said, "Well, he can't get to any of his classes, and if you're not going to accept our telephone solution, sorry, but that's too bad."

So for two years, during what would have been my junior and senior years of high school, I stayed home. I couldn't reach my classes at the old school, and the best I could do was wait for the new school to be built. At least then I'd have just one flight of stairs to deal with—somehow.

Once the new school was built, my parents offered to carry me up to the second floor when needed, but I told them no; I had friends who could carry me and my wheelchair up and down the stairs.

So that's what we did, for two years, and it was not without incident, I might add.

One day, two friends were with me, Bill Malchow in front and Gerald Kersey behind, and they were pulling and pushing me up the stairs in my wheelchair, one step at a time. Suddenly, someone lost his footing and let go of the chair. The chair, Gerald, and I all fell down the stairs, and ran over Bill, who had been in front of me. It's a wonder it didn't kill me or my friends or at least completely destroy the chair, but it didn't. We picked ourselves up, took the chair to a bicycle shop, and asked them whether the bent frame, broken spokes, and flat tires could be repaired. It took a couple of days, but my chair was resurrected, I went back to school, and I went back up those steps.

By the time I graduated, I was 21 years old. Because I'd missed two years, I had to cram four years of English and literature into my final two years. To make up for lost time, I went to summer school, sometimes going to other districts because my own school didn't offer a particular course.

All because the school wouldn't put in a simple elevator.

That's not to say I had no education during the two years off. I learned a great deal, albeit not in the traditional way. For one thing, I devoured all kinds of magazines, particularly *Popular Science* and *Popular Mechanics*. I was fascinated by how people could turn ideas into real mechanical things, how things fit together, and how things worked. These magazines were my textbooks, and I kept every single issue, even memorized them—so much so that years later, I could recall what was on a single page from a single issue.

I was also spending quite a bit of time with my mother's seven brothers, who were all mechanical gurus and gearheads. They were truck drivers and car mechanics, mostly. Everywhere you looked, they had cars, trucks, stock cars, motorcycles, and all manner of automotive parts. Most people would look at the combination of things they had accumulated and say it was junk, but that's not how my uncles saw it. To them, those parts were pieces of a puzzle that hadn't been put together yet. To me, it was a playground, a Disneyworld of motors and metal.

My uncles also used to do a lot of work out at the house of their parents, my Grandma and Grandpa Freeman. A common sight under a shade tree was them pulling the motor out of a pickup truck and sticking something else back in to take its place. Maybe they would be working on a stock car and tuning it up so they could drive it in a race on an old dirt track. They created incredible things. Today, their inventions would be made into patents and sold, but back then, they did it for fun and because it interested them.

I would say I got most of my mechanical aptitude from my mother's side of the family. In fact, if something was broken at our house or if the refrigerator needed leveling, my mom did it, not my dad. He didn't really have the patience to take the time to figure it out and would defer to my mom. My father's side of the family had horses, pigs, cows, dirt, corn, and beans. That's what they knew. So back on the farm, my mother and her brothers would be the ones who fixed things.

A Harvard professor, Howard Gardner, has developed the theory of multiple intelligences, which states that human intelligence should not be measured in just one way (for example, you have an IQ number, and that's it). Rather, there are at least seven categories of intelligence: linguistic, logical-mathematical, musical, bodily kinesthetic, spatial, interpersonal, and intrapersonal. According to Gardner, the seven intelligences operate at the same time and not independently, complementing each other in a unique blend that helps individuals develop skills, solve problems, and play their roles in life. While all people possess each of these intelligences in some amount, they are usually stronger in some areas than others. For instance, whereas my uncles and mother might have been strong in logical-mathematical, bodily kinesthetic, and spatial intelligences, my father excelled in linguistic, interpersonal, and intrapersonal intelligences. Hopefully, I have equal parts of both of them inside me.

Another way to illustrate the differences between my mom and dad involves one story about a motorized wagon and another about a horse.

In the first story, my uncles had taken an old one-cylinder, gasoline-powered washing machine motor and attached it to a wood wagon with the idea that we could all ride it around the yard and have some fun. They mostly did it for my benefit, and let me tell you, it was a big deal to me. You had to kick-start it, like a motorcycle, and then someone would give it a good push to get it going. You sat inside it, like a Radio Flyer wagon, and steered as it took off. Because it didn't have a brake, the only way to stop was for someone to run alongside the wagon and grab you so you could slow down.

In the second story, when we were still living at the nursery and farm, my dad rented a pony for me to ride one summer. Every so often, my dad would take me down to the barn we kept the pony in, saddle up the pony, and put me on it. I'd ride around the little barnyard. Then, on the first day of school, my mom gave me a bath and a haircut and dressed me in nice, new clothes so I would look presentable. By that point, I'd been riding the pony all summer and wanted one more ride before my father returned it. I begged my dad, as kids do, for one last ride, and he gave in. He put me on the pony, like he always did, and then all of a sudden, it took off running. Something must have spooked it, or maybe it knew its days on the farm were numbered, because it ran full speed through the cornfield. It was the beginning of the school year, so the corn was almost fully grown. I held on for dear life and had absolutely no control over the pony. Finally, it dumped me off, except my leg got caught in the stirrup. Instead of the pony just running away, it dragged me for about 50 feet through the wet corn and dirt. When my dad finally caught up, the pony had stopped, and I was a mess. Back in the house, my mother had to go through the whole bath and clothes routine all over again. I missed the bus, and they had to drive me to school. In 1947, this was not easy because the roads were bad, school was five miles away, and we had a 10-year-old jalopy.

In those two stories lay the seeds of my future. One side of the family gave me a motor and the other, a pony; when you put them together, you get horsepower. Though I never rode a pony again, I've got one heck of a story, thanks to my dad.

During the two years I spent out of school, my mind raced with possibilities. I spent a lot of time in the garage while I played with motors that were similar to the ones my uncles had used. I hooked belts up to them, studied how they worked, and noted the effect they had on other things.

I also spent a lot of time using a little buzz box welder that my dad had bought at an auction sale. I plugged it into an outlet in the garage, and with some scrap metal my uncles had given me, I taught myself how to weld.

I was amazed that I could take two pieces of metal and, using welding rods and electricity, stick them together to make anything

I wanted. I liked seeing the sparks flying and feeling the heat radiating. I also made things out of wood, but I found out early on that I was a metal guy; for me, there was no fun in sawdust.

The garage was my laboratory. While my classmates studied theoretical physics in school, I applied those theories in our garage.

Proving that the apple did not fall far from the entrepreneurial tree, just as my mom and dad had gone into business for themselves as Marathon distributors, I started making things at home and then selling them. I made cake pans, small lamps, rabbits, and yard decorations that had a little guy standing and watering a plant with a can. I made nativity scenes out of plywood and painted all of these things in the house. As I said, I wasn't a wood guy, but I used wood when it made sense; somehow it seemed logical to make nativity scenes out of wood.

Attached to the house was an unheated room I would use for my workshop, but in the winter, I worked in my mother's kitchen, with the paint and sawdust flying everywhere. My mother helped me by bringing me saber saws, jigsaws, paint, and brushes. When the smell, noise, and sawdust got too bad, I had to go out into the back room, heat or no heat. I could no longer walk at that point, so I pushed myself around the house in an office chair.

In those days, decorating a home at Christmas was a big matter of pride. Because my items were all made out of nice wood with my own craftsmanship, instead of plastic, like things made in China that you might see today, I knew people would like them. To sell them, I created a display in our yard. I shone a spotlight on it so passersby could envision how the items might look outside their own homes. At first, people would stop and ask where we got the items so they could go buy them themselves. After I told them I made them, they started buying from me, even placing orders for the following year.

The nativity scenes were popular, but when I started making yard rabbits, business really multiplied—pardon the pun. I'd make families of them, with a mom and pop rabbit and their little bunnies. I must have made at least 25 families of them, and I easily sold them all. Getting money for this was nice, but it was not my goal.

The truth is I got great pleasure out of seeing somebody else enjoying something I'd crafted with my own two hands. I had heard the comments from ignorant people long enough: "Well, you're going to live on government money the rest of your life" and "You're going to be a burden on your parents." More than anything, I wanted to prove that I could be a contributing member of society, not just in terms of the money I could make but in terms of the satisfaction I could provide through my handiwork. The money was a by-product and perhaps evidence that if I gave to society, society would give back to me.

Finally, like any good education, life during this time was not all work. One thing comes to mind in this regard.

No matter what my prognosis was, I always felt like I could beat it. To prove it to myself, I had my dad hang a bag full of sand in the garage so I could use it as a punching bag. I thought that if I beat the bag up, I could keep my arms and muscles strong, and as long as I did that, I'd be OK. Sitting on my stool and wailing away at that bag, I was certainly no Rocky Marciano, but I gave it everything I had. Maybe it was my form of physical education. In the long run, I'm not sure whether it did me any good. Some doctors say it could have used up whatever finite amount of energy my muscles had stored inside of them and hastened their deterioration. Other doctors say the activity could have strengthened them and helped to prevent a more rapid loss. Who's to say? I will say this: that bag took an awful lot of abuse from me, and it gave out long before I did.

chapter five

MOON SHOTS

*We choose to go to the moon in this decade and
do the other things, not because they are easy,
but because they are hard.*

-- John F. Kennedy

In 1961, one year before I graduated from high school, President John F. Kennedy said the United States would land a man on the moon.

Speaking before a joint session of Congress, he said, "First, I believe that this nation should commit itself to achieving the goal, before this decade is out, of landing a man on the moon and returning him back safely to earth. No single space project in this period will be more impressive to mankind or more important for the long-range exploration of space, and none will be so difficult or expensive to accomplish."

When Kennedy said this, only one Soviet, Yuri Gagarin, had ever gone into orbit, and just one American, Alan Shepard, had flown in space—for 15 minutes and 28 seconds, only one month earlier. To people of all ages, this was a time of excitement and possibility. If even the sky itself was not the limit, what did the future hold for us? Put simply, you didn't have to be a rocket scientist to know this was an ambitious goal.

Did Kennedy's moon shot inspire me to great things? Did it propel me to launch my company? It did other members of my generation, so the convenient or politically correct answer would be yes. I could say the combination of scientific discovery and human potential filled me with a romantic notion that anything was possible if I put my mind to it. While that's partly true, the authentic answer is really no, Kennedy's moon shot did not inspire me in that way. That doesn't mean I wasn't proud of my country; I was, and I am. After all, in those days, we were in a race with the Soviet Union, and I was happy to have a leg up on them.

My thoughts were more down to earth.

When Kennedy gave his speech in 1961, most people my age were concerned with what they were going to be when they grew up. My concern was that I wanted to grow up, period. Their concern was what they were going to do, whether they were going to be farmers like their dads or drive fire trucks. I never thought about those things. I thought about being alive. That was my total focus. Consequently, I never really considered how bad it was or how bad it could get some day. It never crossed my mind that I may not survive. I just wanted to live every day as much as I possibly could.

Staying alive was my moon shot.

I can recall when I was 12 years old and still able to walk. I would go to the altar of my church and pray to God that he would perform a miracle that I would no longer be disabled. I have to say that miracle did happen—he blessed me with the ability to take care of myself and help others. My prayers were answered.

However, in those days, I wasn't above getting a little extra heavenly insurance.

For instance, when I was still in Catholic school, I'd get up and walk to church on Saturday mornings in the spring. Why would I do that when getting around was so hard for me? Was I that much of a fervent believer? Well, I did have a strong faith, but I also knew you got big brownie points with the nuns if you went to church on Saturday mornings. I mean, I wasn't the best student in the world, and I figured I needed every bit of help I could get. A few other brownnosed kids were there, but to me, going to church on Saturday was like spiritual rocket fuel with the nuns.

It was hard work—an ordeal. As spring became summer, I began to notice I couldn't make it all the way to church and back without stopping to rest about three-quarters of the way home. After a short rest, I'd finish the trip. As the year wore on, I stopped more frequently, making it halfway and then a quarter of the way. After a while, I seemed to be doing more resting than walking. I'd leave the church, go down the stairway, cross the street, and sit on a stone wall. At the courthouse, I'd sit on the steps. In between stops, people would pull up next to me in their cars and ask whether I wanted a ride home. I always said no, that I was OK. One day, when I couldn't take another step, I had to ask someone to call my mother. I knew, and my parents knew, that the inevitable was going to happen and I wasn't going to be able to walk anymore, and not just to church.

Unbeknownst to me, my aunt and my cousin, who had multiple sclerosis, asked the Multiple Sclerosis Society in Fort Wayne whether they would give me a wheelchair and deliver it to my house. They did, and I was not happy. I figured that once I gave in to what I called "The Iron Monster", I'd never get out. I thought I was finished.

The chair sat in the house for quite some time before I would even acknowledge its presence. One day when we were going to go somewhere as a family, my father finally said, "Well, I think we better fold this thing up and stick it in the trunk so you can get around when we get there." I said, "If nobody that I know sees me, I'll do it." I knew inside that if I didn't accept my situation, it was going to be really tough on my parents and everybody around me. It wasn't that I thought the wheelchair had a stigma; to me, the jig was up, and it was a sign of the end.

Reluctantly, I gave in to the wheelchair.

Inspiration comes in all shapes and sizes, and I drew some of it, indirectly, from a local man named Virgil Reinbarger, who was the only person I'd seen at that time who could be called "disabled." Virgil had a mild case of polio and used to work for nearby farmers by dragging himself from place to place on his crutches. I remember watching him and thinking, "Hey, he's 40 years old, and he's making it through life OK. Why can't it be OK for me? There's no reason I can't do what he does."

If that wasn't enough to impress me, Virgil then upped the ante: he started riding around in a motorcycle with a sidecar. Let me tell you, I thought that was the coolest thing. A disabled James Dean right there in Winamac. I watched him do this for years, and then one day I remember thinking, "Maybe I could make something I could ride around on, just like Virgil."

In the world of inventors and entrepreneurs, this is the moment of inspiration, the flash of an idea that, if properly executed, can change the world. For me, however, changing the world would have to wait just a little while longer.

In the spring of 1962, I graduated from high school and prepared to get on with life. I could not—would not—sit at home and wait for others to take care of me, no matter what society thought I would or should do. My mother went to college, so I thought I would do the same. Over the next six months, I applied to several schools in Indiana and was met with the same wall of resistance: no one wanted a guy in a wheelchair who was trying to get an education.

Linda Keys, my girlfriend, who would later become my wife, was going to Indiana State University in Terre Haute. During some of my visits to see her, I wondered whether I could also attend the school—I was concerned not about the academics but about campus access for someone in a wheelchair. It seemed within my reach, so I applied and was accepted for the first semester of 1963. I'd be going to the school where the legendary John Wooden had once coached basketball before going to UCLA and where Larry Bird would later become an All-American before starting his Hall of Fame career with the Boston Celtics.

My goal was not nearly as high. To me, going to college was merely the next thing to do if you were going to be a success in the world.

A classmate and I worked out a deal where he could stay in my dorm room for free if he helped me around campus. While that arrangement was good in theory, in practice it ended up not being feasible. For one thing, our class schedules were different and required us to be in different places at different times. For another, whether he was with me or not, accessibility was an ongoing issue.

Like high school, the university was not set up to accommodate someone in a wheelchair, except now it was even worse. There were multiple sets of stairs in buildings set far apart. The few elevators they had were not in spots where I needed them. As a consequence, I had to use service elevators that required a special key. Getting in and out of buildings was hard because there were no curb cuts or ramps. I had to use alleys and back entrances. The narrow walkways between buildings, if they were paved, were also not well cared for and were certainly not suited for wheelchairs.

Trying to get around the grounds of the college was mentally and physically exhausting. If I made it to class at all, I was usually late, which didn't go over too well with professors. Once I got there, it was no easy task to find a place to park myself where I could adequately see and hear without disrupting the class.

The decision to leave school after one semester was easy. I wish it didn't have to be so, but continuing any further was virtually impossible for me. By the summer of 1963, I was done. So was Linda, who had also decided she wasn't going to go back to Indiana State. At home in Winamac, with a marriage on the horizon, it was time to start making a living.

With the knowledge of bookkeeping and numbers I'd gained from working with my mother on my little craft-making business, I got a job running a Burrows posting machine on the third shift at Logansport Hospital. From 11 p.m. to 7 a.m., my job was to post daily charges to patients for rooms and other expenses. Because I worked next to the emergency room entrance, I had another duty. Every time an ambulance pulled up to the entrance of the hospital, the emergency room bell rang. This meant that I had to go from my bookkeeping machine to the door in my manual wheelchair and let the emergency medical technicians and the patients inside. Once they were in the waiting room, I then had to admit them, which meant filling out forms on a typewriter, with their names, addresses, next of kin, Social Security numbers, and so on. It was pretty hectic, and I could tell that trying to get around in a manual wheelchair was not going to be a long-term solution for me. I began thinking in earnest about how I could make a motorized wheelchair.

After saving a bit of money, I started venturing out to look for parts to build a scooter. I'd get out of work at 7 a.m., have someone load my manual wheelchair in my Chevrolet, and drive to my buddy Gerald Kersey's house in Winamac. Then we would drive to places like Elkhart and Galveston, in Indiana; White Pigeon, in Michigan; and Chicago, where I would buy parts—

designing and building the scooter in my head—and then bring the stuff back to Winamac.

Because most of these parts suppliers were at least two hours away and I didn't exactly know what I was looking for until I found it, this search for and purchase of parts took most of the day. As Gerald drove back to Winamac, I tried to sleep in the car. Once I was home, I'd get a little more rest, clean up, and go back to work at the hospital. I did this every day for two straight months and worked on my days off to put the pieces together. The routine was grueling, but I was fueled by the idea that one day I would have a motorized scooter that would make my life a lot easier.

I badly needed the money I got from my job, but I was getting run down. Finally, one Saturday night at the hospital helped me make the decision to leave. Because of a serious car accident, in which two sisters had just been killed on a highway, the emergency room was filled with a family in complete despair. The family members were hysterical and needed to be admitted quickly so a doctor could prescribe sedatives for them. Seeing people in such distress was gut-wrenching. The next morning, when my supervisor came in, I told him that I was burned out and couldn't do it anymore.

In the two months I worked at Logansport Hospital, after driving to and from parts suppliers during the day and working in a garage during my spare hours, I had somehow cobbled together my first scooter. In today's parlance, it would be called something like Release 1.0 or the iChair. I didn't care what it was called because I knew that life—at least my life—would never again be the same.

To put that in perspective, let's go back to President Kennedy and outer space.

To land a man on the moon and bring him back safely in the years between 1961 and 1969 took immediate technological creativity and $25 billion in resources, which equates to $150 billion today—a lot to ask of a nation in peacetime. At its apex, the Apollo program employed 400,000 people and 20,000 industrial firms and universities. It required no less than a national mobilization.

Though I didn't think of it this way at the time, in retrospect, building my first motorized wheelchair in the summer of 1963 was no less of a moon shot.

If you think this is hyperbole, consider the following: I was 22 years old, I worked alone and got little sleep, I used money I'd saved from working at the hospital and making and selling crafts, and my work space consisted of my mother's kitchen and the garage in our backyard. I had no connections, no economics degree from Harvard or Yale, and no fancy business plan. I was confined to a wheelchair at a time when society looked at people like me with everything from pity to scorn—if they looked at us at all.

Do I think my life would have been better if I hadn't been afflicted with spinal muscular atrophy? No, I don't at all. I was frustrated then—and sometimes now I am, too—because of certain things I couldn't do for myself. I'd rather I didn't need help going to the restroom, taking a shower, or eating. It would be easier to pick up my own drill than to try to tell somebody to drill a 3/8 hole instead of a 5/16 hole. But I have learned to handle those frustrations and deal with them because that's the way it is. I know I have more to offer to society than just sitting around and worrying about a few frustrations and my own discomfort. To do otherwise seems self-indulgent and wrong.

No, dealing with my disability was the easy part. Building that first motorized wheelchair? Now, that's where the story gets interesting.

chapter six

ADVENTURES IN MACHINE MAKING

There are no constraints on the human mind, no walls around the human spirit, no barriers to our progress except those we erect for ourselves.

-- Ronald Reagan

TO SAY my first motorized wheelchair was a "scooter" is like calling Frankenstein a munchkin.

Created in my parents' garage out of a mish-mash of nuts, bolts, wires, tires, and other unrelated machine parts, the vehicle was a four-wheeled monster. It was big and loud and dirty and smelly, and it tore up everything in its path, including my mother's kitchen, where I first drove it to show her my creation.

To build this beast, I started with a Crosley CC, which was a small four-cylinder car made in the '40s and '50s. I cut its front end down to 24 inches wide, added a lawn mower differential, four big wheel-barrow tires, two six-volt automotive batteries, makeshift wiring and switches I got from the hardware store, a kitchen chair, and a motor from a 1957 Pontiac kid's car that I rescued from a mortician's trash bin. Then, like a mad scientist, I welded, screwed, bolted, and hammered it all together.

When you consider that the machine had two six-volt batteries and did not have variable speeds, which meant it went either 7.5 miles per hour or 15 miles per hour, could not go in reverse, and also had no brakes, it was like a hopped-up Frankenstein on steroids. If you were at full throttle and going down a hill or a ramp or you were in a tight area, like my mother's kitchen, it was bad news for whatever was in your way. Many times, while trying to maneuver, I burned rubber on my mother's floor, rammed into her refrigerator, cabinets, and sink, and busted through the door.

It was a crude device, but creating it gave me hope that I could build something out of nothing and make it work. Despite the wreckage I caused to her kitchen, my mother was also happy, as was my father. They saw I was making progress and it was only a matter of time before I'd get what I wanted.

Starting with the body of a Crosley was fitting. For one thing, I was a big race fan, and before the Chevrolet Corvette started competing in 1956, the Crosley Hotshot had been America's only sports car. It was very competitive in its class, winning the Sebring, the Grand de la Suisse, and the Sports Car Club of America's 12-hour Vero Beach race in 1951. In the same year, the Hotshot also finished second in the Tokyo Grand Prix and was headed to victory at Le Mans when its voltage regulator caught fire near the end of the race.

What's more, the Crosley was manufactured locally, in Marion, Indiana, by automotive pioneer Powell Crosley Jr. A visionary, Crosley made the first mass-market single overhead camshaft engine, the first American car with four-wheel disc brakes, the first slab-sided post-War car, and the first all-steel-bodied wagon. Though Crosley was out of business by 1952, luminaries such as Humphrey Bogart, Gloria Swanson, and New York Governor Nelson Rockefeller all drove the cars.

As for racing, my love of the sport remained strong throughout my life. Like chips off the old engine block, my sons, Todd, Brent, and Drew, also loved it, too, racing go-karts and midgets when they were little boys. Since 2002, Todd has owned Braun Racing, a very competitive team in the NASCAR Nationwide Series. Based in Mooresville, North Carolina, Braun Racing is in the very heart of NASCAR country.

Back when I was creating my first motorized wheelchair in the summer of 1963, my interest in racing and the Crosley's pedigree were the furthest things from my mind. I was a young man on a mission, and to me the Crosley's long-abandoned body was just another metallic piece of the puzzle I would need on my way to making a more refined "scooter."

As soon as Frankenstein was finished, I started working on the Bride of Frankenstein, the second version of my motorized wheel-chair. After wrecking my mother's kitchen with the first version, I decided I needed to make the second version much smaller and more manageable. This meant using three wheels instead of four, finding a way to make variable speeds, and adding brakes, better steering, and a host of other improvements. It also meant I needed to go beyond the local parts I'd been using and start traveling to places, such as Chicago and White Pigeon, that had more appro-priate materials for what I was trying to accomplish.

The question was, What should I look for? I couldn't use the Internet to do research, so I bought surplus catalogs for a dollar and a half and studied them, as well as whatever books and maga-zines I could get my hands on. Those publications became my library, and I spent hour after hour with them. I read, I contem-plated, I schemed. I would think of a challenge I'd faced while building and testing Frankenstein, and then I'd try to figure out what parts I could procure that might address that challenge. While sitting quietly alone, either in the garage or in the house, I'd painstakingly put those pieces together in my head and try every kind of configuration possible. More times than not, these configurations led me down dark alleys and dead ends, and I'd have to start again. All the stops and starts were frustrating, but they were also necessary because they were part of the process of discovery.

I remember reading once that Thomas Edison said, "I have not failed; I have just found 10,000 ways that won't work." I also recall Albert Einstein saying he owed much of his success to his ability to sit quietly for hours on end, thinking. I will never claim to be Edison or Einstein, but experience has taught me that a lot can be said for quiet contemplation. For one thing, by the time you actually start trying to execute your vision and build something, the move from theoretical to practical brings a whole new set of challenges, and it's far better to have already thought it through before you get there.

One of my biggest challenges was figuring out how to give my machine the ability to travel at variable speeds. Like many discoveries, I found that solution almost by accident. While building Frankenstein, I had seen an advertisement for a one-person golf cart that was built and sold in California. Of course, it was far too expensive for me to purchase.

All was not lost, however. In the process of investigating the golf carts, I discovered the carts' motor manufacturer, Gillette Manufacturing, was in White Pigeon, Michigan. I found the company's number, called and spoke with the owner, Paul Gillette, and arranged to go to Michigan to get one of his motors.

As soon as I arrived, I was struck by his generosity. When I told him I needed to learn how to make a motor with variable speeds, he taught me. He could have just sold me the motor and told me to get lost, but he didn't. Instead, he told me how he'd taken an old Ford generator, rewound its fields, and put more connections on it to make it reversible. Then he demonstrated how to wind varying lengths of wire into a coil, put the wire across some solenoids, and run current through it to make variable speeds. This was a huge discovery for me. I went back to Winamac with a motor and a very valuable piece of knowledge.

Another challenge I faced was the size of my tires. I wanted to drive my vehicle everywhere—the street, the sidewalk, inside buildings, you name it—so I needed to use something considerably smaller than wheelbarrow tires.

In those days, go-karts were all the rage, especially in race-crazy Indiana, where little boys dreamed of being the next A. J. Foyt, a four-time winner of the Indianapolis 500. Invented in 1956 by Art Ingels, a race car designer and engineer at Kurtis Craft, a firm that produced five Indy 500 winners, go-karts were essentially race cars for kids. For a young inventor like me, I saw promise in the go-karts' small, semipneumatic tires, so I started looking for some.

One day, while reading a go-kart magazine, I saw an advertisement for the Maple Grove Distributing Company, which sold minibikes and go-karts in Galveston, Indiana, just south of Logansport. I decided I'd go see what they had in the way of go-kart tires.

That's when I encountered Ralph Rocky, a tall drink of water with a severe facial tic, which may very well have been Tourette's syndrome, a neurological disorder. We bonded instantly, seeming to communicate telepathically, each knowing what the other was going to say before it was even said. In the same way that Paul Gillette would become a mentor to me, so would Ralph Rocky.

On that first day I met Ralph, I told him what I was trying to build and the tires I thought I needed, and I asked whether he had any other parts I might be able to use. He had a retail store in the front of the building and a mail-order business in the back. With just a vague hint from me, Ralph went into his back room and returned with a collection of things that he spread out on the counter. I was like a kid on Christmas morning who was seeing his presents for the first time. Besides the go-kart tires, he brought some smaller differentials he purchased off a lawn mower shop that had closed. He had about 100 of them, and though they were already better than the differential I'd used on Frankenstein, the lengths of the axles were still not right. I bought one anyway, thinking I could make it smaller once I got it home. I also bought some tubing and motorcycle pegs to rest my feet on. Then I took it all back to the garage and started welding it together.

Frankenstein's Bride was finished at summer's end in 1963. She wasn't pretty, but she had three wheels and was a lot better looking than Frankenstein. More important, she had a lot better temper.

The week after I finished my new three-wheeled scooter, my mother got an important phone call from our neighbor. The Controls Company of America plant in Winamac was going to have a job opening for a quality control inspector, and if I wanted to apply for it, I'd better get over there. How did our neighbor know? It was her son's job, and he'd just enlisted in the armed services.

Before my mother could hang up the phone, I said I'd get on my new scooter and ride over to the company. Our neighbor then called the manager of the factory and spoke with his secretary, Doris Dilts, to let him know I was on my way. I was indeed on my way, in more ways than one.

When I got there, I faced the usual obstacle of access: steps and no ramp. Luckily, I did find an entranceway to the cafeteria. I went in and asked someone to tell the manager I was there to talk about the job. A couple of minutes later, the plant manager and Ben Severns, the guy who would eventually be my boss, came out to see me. They stood there, looking at me sitting on Frankenstein's Bride, and they were dumbfounded. Here's how the conversation went:

"What is this thing?" they asked.

"It's a motorized wheelchair," I replied.

"Where did you get it?" they asked.

"I built it," I said.

"No, really," they said. "What company sells these?"

"No company," I said. "I built it myself."

"What do you mean?" they asked. "Did you have a kit that you sent away for?"

"No, I got a bunch of different parts from up in Michigan and Illinois and down in Galveston and some other local supply stores, and then I put it all together," I said. "I just finished it last week, as a matter of fact."

"Last week?" they asked, incredulously. "And you drove it over here?"

"Yes, about six or seven blocks," I said. "And there was no kit. I figured it all out in my head."

"In your head?" they asked.

"That's right," I said. "This is my second one. The first one was a monster. I'm getting better at it now."

They looked back and forth at each other and at me. They rubbed their chins while walking around my chair.

"Hell, if you can do that, you can do the job we've got open. No sweat."

We shook hands, and on the first day of October 1963, I was hired on the spot for $1.46 per hour, full time. The company made automotive switches that turned the lights on and off when car doors opened and closed. My job was to inspect all the materials that went into the products and make sure they met the proper specifications. Looking back, having just built a couple of motorized wheelchairs out of nothing, I realize this job was somewhat beneath my abilities. However, in 1963, nobody was hiring disabled people, and to even get someone to think about giving you a job, you had to vastly overachieve, which I had done. I didn't think about it that way; I was happy to have a job. Once again, all I wanted was to be like everyone else.

So I had a job. To get to and from work, I drove Frankenstein's Bride on the streets, in all kinds of weather. As the months wore on and the weather got colder, I put on more layers of clothing. I also installed a flashing red light on a pole that rose above my head so people could see me through the dark and rain and snow. I must have made quite a sight as I slipped and slid and shivered on my way to and from work. Because there were no sidewalks I could ride on, at first I was concerned that I would be in people's way on the streets. I figured they'd be irritated that I was going so slowly, but the opposite happened. Honking, waving, and calling out with appreciation as they drove by, they actually looked out for me.

A few weeks after I got my job, I was faced with another obstacle. I was going to get married in December, and I did not want to have my new wife living with me in my parents' home. Because I made only $1.46 per hour and had just started my job, I began looking at mobile homes because I thought they would be a lot more affordable.

The first mobile home I looked at was a New Moon, which was very popular in those days. It didn't work for me because I needed the doorways and hallway to be wider so I could have room for my chair. Because New Moons were built on an assembly line, with no room for deviation, I had to look for an off-make model. I found Venus Coaches, a small manufacturer in Nappanee, Indiana, and convinced them to custom-make a mobile home for me and deliver it to a trailer park in Logansport—by December. In addition to the short turnaround, there were two problems. First, since they were selling it to me directly instead of through a dealer, I'd have to set it up myself, and I had no idea how to do that. Second, it would cost me $3,300, which to me was a king's ransom.

In the same way that I was overcoming physical obstacles, I was also finding my way around financial roadblocks. I did not have the money to buy my mobile home, and banks were not exactly open to the idea of lending to a guy in a wheelchair, so I got my father to cosign a loan for me. I was buying my first home.

On the day I got married, December 28, 1963, Linda and I went to the trailer for the first time, ready to start our new life together. What did we find? There was no water because the pipes had frozen solid.

For the next few hours, my cousins and friends crawled around under the trailer with heat tapes, insulation wraps, and blowtorches as they tried to thaw the place out. My wife sat inside and forlornly looked out the window. I felt bad while I sat on my motorized wheelchair and "supervised" while my buddies, also in their suits, nearly froze to death.

Two weeks later, the sewage pipe became frozen and fell off, causing raw sewage to run all over the yard. Once again, my friends and cousins came to my rescue, as they swam in filthy sewage and worked to thaw and reconnect my sewage pipes.

It was an inauspicious beginning to my new life. Always the optimist, I figured it had to get better. Didn't it?

chapter seven

CHANGING TIMES

*The thing that lies at the foundation of
positive change, the way I see it, is service to a
fellow human being.*

-- Lee Iacocca

BY THE year 1964, change was everywhere.

In business, IBM introduced its S/360 mainframe computer, a technological marvel that would enable the company to dominate the business world for decades. That same year, the first Ford Mustang rolled off a Dearborn, Michigan, assembly line, and within two years, Ford would sell more than 1 million units, thus making it one of the most successful product launches in automotive history.

Social upheaval was also in the air. President Kennedy had been assassinated in November of 1963. The Civil Rights Act of 1964 was passed, and the stage was set for the Voting Rights Act of 1965 the following year. In another harbinger of change, President Lyndon B. Johnson signed the Gulf of Tonkin Resolution, which authorized him, without a formal declaration of war by Congress, to use military force in Southeast Asia.

The change for me was much more prosaic, but it was there. I was a newlywed, in my first home, with a mortgage and my first real job. My wife also had a job working as a long-distance operator for the phone company, and having two incomes was nice.

However, because our trailer was in Logansport, which was a 30-minute car ride to my job in Winamac, getting to and from work was going to be a real problem. Bundling up to drive through the sleet and snow for six or eight blocks on my scooter was manageable, but it was not practical or safe to do it from Logansport, even in perfect weather. I had to come up with a workable solution.

First, I worked out a deal with a man named George Moise, the owner of a filling station in Winamac that was right across the street from my job as a quality control inspector. Each day after work, I would drive my scooter across the street to George's station and leave it there overnight so he could charge the battery. Then I'd fill up the old gas-guzzling Chevy Impala that I'd bought and drive home to Logansport. Once there, I used my manual wheelchair in the house. The next day, I'd drive the Impala back to George's station in Winamac, pick up my freshly charged scooter, and ride it across the street to work.

Still, I needed to be more mobile at home and on weekends, and without access to my motorized scooter, it was very hard. My solution? I invented a rack—kind of like the bicycle racks you see today, but in those days they had not been invented yet—that attached to the back of the Impala and held my motorized chair. It wasn't pretty, but it did the job. However, I still felt like I could come up with a better solution.

At this point, I started working on the next version of my scooter. For the first time, instead of holding the design in my head,

I began making detailed drawings. I had taken drafting in school, I had the necessary blueprints and other materials, and because I had a full-time job, I had time on the weekends to devote to the project. I also began to get the idea that I'd be making more than one, and because of that, a blueprint seemed like a good thing to have. In fact, I knew I'd make at least one more because I wanted to have one at home, as well as one at work. The idea just might work because enough people were talking to me about my scooter that I thought I might have an opportunity to make more.

Needing materials to make this third version of my scooter, I went back to Paul Gillette and Ralph Rocky, my two main parts suppliers. They sold me the same parts at the same price, and it was easy—I had one scooter at home and one at work. This increased mobility also had some side benefits: not only was having two scooters more convenient but also more people saw me on my scooter because I rode it around on weekends and evenings. Each time I showed up riding my scooter, people would come over and start asking questions. This was particularly true the day I went to a social function at a church near Logansport, where I got my very first customer.

A boy at this church had the Duchenne form of muscular dystrophy, and he and his family were really struggling to help him have a normal life. After seeing me on my scooter, the family began talking among themselves about how nice it would be to have one for their son. A woman elder at the church overheard their conversation and privately asked me how much it would cost for them to buy one from me. Remembering how much the one I was riding on at that time cost me to build, I told her I could do it for $300: $150 for parts and $150 for labor. That's when we made the deal. She said the church would take up a collection and pay me on delivery.

This is when I learned one very big lesson about business: if you don't price your product or service right, you won't be in business for very long. It's not greed or the desire to take advantage of people; it's strictly a fact of business. I learned this rather obvious piece of knowledge from my usual "business school" teachers, Ralph and Paul. When I went back to them to purchase the parts to make this first customer's chair, they told me the actual price was going to be higher than what they'd charged me the previous times. They explained that they'd sold the parts to me at a reduced price because they wanted to do me a favor, but if I was going to start turning around and using those parts to make a business, well, that was a different story. As a result, this first customer's scooter took me two weeks to build, and I didn't make a penny.

In the end, what I did have was a product—I called it the "Tri-Wheeler"—experience, and the satisfaction of helping someone.

I can recall delivering the Tri-Wheeler to the boy and his family like it was yesterday. The woman elder at the church had arranged a Saturday carry-in dinner so the whole congregation could come and present the Tri-Wheeler as a surprise. It was very emotional because neither the boy nor his family had any idea that this was going to happen.

I brought the Tri-Wheeler to the church on the back of my Impala, using the rack. When we presented the Tri-Wheeler to the boy and his family, they gasped and stared, slack-jawed. Then we put the boy on the Tri-Wheeler and watched as he began to drive it, tentatively at first but then with increasing confidence. For the first time in his life, he could move around without somebody pushing him. The whole experience was incredibly liberating for him—but not so much for his parents, who said, "My God, we're going to lose our son. We're not sure this is such a good thing."

This dichotomy between independence and loss is a common occurrence with our customers and their families. It was certainly the case with this first family. The boy was 10 years old, and his parents had spent every waking moment pushing him around so he could get from one place to the next. All of a sudden, as if with a snap of the fingers, he was mobile. He was free to explore the world. The feeling is somewhat akin to when parents give up their car keys to their teenagers for the first time. However, in the case of this boy and millions of others like him, this gift of mobility is much more poignant.

Though I didn't make any money on the first Tri-Wheeler sale, it was very satisfying. For years afterward, every time I heard a story about how the boy used the scooter at school and at home and what freedom it gave him, I said a quiet thanks and felt my heart fill with blessings.

However, no matter how spiritually satisfying my first sale was, I remembered the lesson I'd learned about pricing accurately. Accordingly, I priced the next scooter at $595. I didn't get rich off of it, but I did gain a small profit and, just as important, the confidence and ability to find more customers.

That next Tri-Wheeler customer was an Indianapolis man by the name of Jim Pauley, who was a hemophiliac and was so obese he couldn't walk. I had met Jim and his wife, who had polio and was also in a wheelchair, at a conference in Indianapolis run by the National Paraplegic Foundation (NPF). The NPF was an organization of wheelchair-bound people who were trying to band together so they could lobby for societal changes such as curb cuts, ramps, and other types of access. Though Jim had the use of his legs and was not technically a paraplegic, he was still confined to a wheelchair and sought the same reforms as his wife and the other lobbyists.

Jim was a good-hearted man with a fighting spirit and was very active in advocating for change in Indianapolis's disabled community. I loved his can-do attitude and determination and heard many stories about how he would wheel himself straight into the mayor of Indianapolis's office without stopping at the receptionist's desk. He acted like he owned the place. If you think about it, he did own the place—as a taxpaying citizen—which meant the mayor, as an elected representative, worked for him.

At the NPF event, Jim asked me whether he could have a Tri-Wheeler like the one I was riding. I said sure, knowing I would have to make some pretty drastic modifications to my own design so the machine could accommodate his weight. I also knew how badly Jim needed the Tri-Wheeler and how much it would impact his life. As a hemophiliac, he had to be very careful not to bump up against things, and especially not to fall, because he would bleed uncontrollably. With the Tri-Wheeler, he would not only be more mobile but also have a lot better chance of controlling his surroundings and protecting himself from dangerous mishaps.

In 1972, Jim became a Tri-Wheeler owner, and he and his wife also purchased one of my wheelchair vans. It was a sky-blue van with a raised roof, raised doors, and a power seat that made it much easier for Jim and his wife to transfer in and out.

The van gave Jim that much more ability to do the things he wanted to do as an advocate for disabled people. He felt the power of mobility in a big way and took it upon himself to be a de facto spokesperson for my company. He promoted our products heavily in the Indianapolis area and with the NPF by driving my vans to their conventions so people could see them, touch them, and go inside of them. He and his wife passed away some years later but not before telling as many people as they could that Braun was a good, solid company to do business with and that we'd helped them immeasurably.

I owe a lot to Jim Pauley, who passed away in 1985. I miss him to this day.

Back in the mid-'60s, other changes were afoot. After a couple of years working as a quality control inspector during the day, making Tri-Wheelers at night and on weekends, and driving to and from our trailer home in Logansport, I had my first child, my daughter, Cherie.

Talk about a blessing. I'd been told I would not live to be a teenager, and not only had I outlived that prediction but also I was a father. I had brought a life into the world, and I was responsible for that life. Moreover, I was as mainstream as a man could get, with a job, a home, and a family. When I held Cherie in my arms and looked into her eyes, what I got back was complete love and acceptance. I was not a person in a wheelchair; I was "Daddy," plain and simple. For all of these things, I felt proud that I was achieving the best that my parents had hoped for me, and above all else, I was grateful to God for giving me such a rich life. I was determined to make the most of what I'd been given.

When Cherie was born and Linda left her job at the phone company, driving back and forth to Logansport became more impractical, so we moved our trailer house back to Winamac and settled in. Once again, I was back on my scooter and riding the eight blocks to work, with my red light flashing, siren sounding, and face and body freezing as I rode through wind, rain, sleet, and snow. I was like the postman, except the only thing I was delivering was myself.

Recently, a visit from one of my old friends, Dave Storey, who I worked with for 10 years at Controls Company, refreshed my memory about a hair-raising experience I had on my scooter while going to work on a cold, blustery winter day. I was asked to work overtime on Saturday but was not told what time to arrive. The factory had installed a very large door to the rear of the plant, to allow fork trucks to enter and exit via a steep ramp. Riding up the ramp, I grabbed the handle of the door and pulled as if it were unlocked, only to discover it was still locked and no one was there yet. I toppled off the edge of the ramp and went sprawling on the cold, dirty ground in the alley. Laying there, freezing, I knew I was in trouble. I started watching out of the corner of my eye to see whether anyone was coming down the sidewalk. Finally, after what seemed like an eternity, a vision appeared before my blood-soaked eyelids, and I screamed out, "Help! Help! Help!" A kind gentleman came running to my assistance, righted my scooter, and found someone else to help get me back on the Tri-Wheeler. The factory was still locked, so I went across the street to the filling station. They let me get in the car wash rack, and we took the hose that was used for washing cars and proceeded to try and clean up my bloodied face and hands. After the cleanup, I sat and waited until I saw others coming to work who could unlock the door, and then I finished my day at work before going home to a very concerned wife. From that time on, when I arrived at work, I immediately made a phone call home to say all was well.

As a family man, I did what family men do: I bought a Bel-Air station wagon. I traded in the old Impala, or, more accurately, put it out of its misery. For one thing, I needed more room for my family and the increasing amount of child-related things that needed to be carted around. For another thing, I wanted to more actively show my Tri-Wheeler to people, and I needed a vehicle with space for my chair.

Another opportunity for change involved my good friend Ralph. By that point, I was making frequent trips to Galveston to buy parts from him because I was making and selling what was then a lot of Tri-Wheelers, at least two or three per month. At this time, my brother-in-law, Ed Heath, was working part time for me building scooters. I would make sales, design the Tri-Wheelers, order parts, go to Galveston to get them, and then bring them back to Winamac. Then Ed would take the parts and build what he could on weeknights. On weekends, we assembled what he'd built. Then I'd deliver them to the customers.

Ralph saw what I was doing and was impressed by my drive and ingenuity; however, he also saw the toll that my schedule was taking on me. One day, he approached me with an interesting proposition: he suggested I move my family to Galveston and help him in his mail-order business while we built Tri-Wheelers in his shop. Because his business was becoming overwhelming to him, he thought he could use my help. He said with the way my mind worked, we could be a great team.

My wife liked this idea and thought it would give us an opportunity to have a house instead of a trailer, but I had problems with it. I already had a full-time job and didn't see the value in exchanging one job for another. Also, as much as I liked Ralph, I felt like I would be giving my business away by building the Tri-Wheelers and selling them through his business.

In spite of my misgivings, my wife and I went to Galveston and began looking at homes, just to see what life might be like down there. In the end, I declined Ralph's offer and decided to stay put. We remained the best of friends, although we lost touch for a couple of years.

The twists and turns of life are amazing—a seemingly small decision can have a major impact. That's one reason why I believe everything has its time and place. While some people may accuse me of going too slowly every now and then, I know I am merely waiting for the right time.

I could have moved to Galveston and worked with Ralph, but who knows what would have happened to my business? Ralph continued to have a deep impact on my life. Exactly how is in itself another story.

chapter eight

OF MENTORS AND MEN

Coming together is a beginning. Keeping together is progress. Working together is success.

-- Henry Ford

ONE OF the things I'm most proud of at Braun is the low turnover rate of our workforce; 40 percent of our employees have been with us for more than 10 years, and nearly a quarter have been with us for more than 15. In this day and age, when people switch jobs as often as they change clothes, that is quite an accomplishment. Is it because Winamac offers fewer opportunities? That could be partly true. However, I think it's more than that.

Every day, our employees make a choice about where they will apply their talents and their passions. They alone decide which company is worthy of their hard work and ingenuity—and they could work anywhere. Like me, they could even start their own businesses. Some could retire. I think our employees stay at Braun because it is a rewarding experience. Our people genuinely enjoy working with each other, and they also appreciate the fact that they are making a difference in so many lives.

I think there is another intangible that makes Braun attractive to our employees. It's not written in any manual, and we have no formal program for it, but I'll bet if you ask our people whether they have a mentor at Braun, they'll say yes. They might not use the term "mentor," but they definitely have people they turn to for advice on how to do things and how to guide their careers.

Braun—and Winamac itself—is a close-knit place. Our people socialize together outside of work and watch out for each other on the job. Because everyone knows everyone so well, each employee is also comfortable enough to challenge another when needed and offer encouragement when times call for it. To be honest, this closeness also comes with its own set of problems; it can sometimes inhibit people from seeking information and points of view from outside their circle of associates. On balance, however, our cohesiveness is a good thing.

Even though I am the company's founder and CEO, I often turn to people for advice. Braun's president, Nick Gutwein, who came to us from Rohm and Haas, is one. Our backgrounds are complementary, and I routinely turn to him for help in my decision making. But it's not just Nick or other members of our senior management team who I see as my mentors. Every time I go to the shop floor and start asking questions, I'm also gathering input I can use to make decisions. In that environment, I feel comfortable enough to simply say "I don't know" and get guidance. In my view, "I don't know" is one of the most powerful things a person can say.

I have been fortunate to have great mentors throughout my life. One of them was the aforementioned Ralph Rocky, the man with the action hero name, to whom I constantly said, "I don't know."

As I noted earlier, Ralph and I had drifted apart but remained close friends after my business had evolved to the point that I no longer needed to purchase my materials from him. We'd stop in and see each other when we were in each other's neck of the woods, but mostly we talked on the phone.

Then one day, Ralph's wife came to see me at my office in Winamac. She told me that Ralph was seriously ill and might die soon. Consequently, Ralph had sent her to ask me whether I would consider buying his business and taking it over. I was making both Tri-Wheelers and wheelchair lifs by that time and had about 50 employees, so I didn't think I could take on that responsibility. I said no. I was flattered and appreciative of all Ralph had done for me, but I didn't feel it was the right choice for me.

His wife was disappointed. She herself was riding a Tri-Wheeler I'd made for her, and she knew the care I put into my work and how hard I worked to market my products. She was with us when Ralph and I went to the Indiana State Fair to sell his lawn mowers, minibikes, and go-karts, as well as my Tri-Wheelers, all in one booth, alongside each other. In addition, I had become adept at my own manufacturing process, and she was aware of that as well.

When she came to visit me, I had moved out of my parents' garage and into my own facility and had different people making different parts all over the place. In fact, a few years earlier I even had some of my employees making lawn mowers for Ralph so I could earn some extra money to pay for the advertisements I was taking out in a magazine called *Accent on Living*. I hadn't realized that I needed to factor the cost of advertising into my products. As a result, the added cost was killing my profits. When I had mentioned it to Ralph, he had an idea that would suit both of us.

Ralph had purchased a factory that manufactured riding lawn mowers that was going out of business in St. Louis. He loaded up several tractor trailers and was storing all the parts in an old schoolhouse in Galveston, but because he lacked the workforce and capability to put it all together, the parts sat there, unused. Today, they'd be called "stranded assets," but to Ralph, they just weren't doing him any good. He asked me to take them home, put them together, and paint them red—Ralph said you could sell anything as long as it was red—and he would pay me for them. He outsourced his manufacturing to me, and I used the extra money to pay for my advertising. It worked for both of us.

But on this particular day, Ralph's wife was there to tell me he was on his deathbed, and I was sorry to have to say no to taking over his business. I was also sad I wouldn't get to see him one last time. I said my silent good-byes.

Over the next few years, my business grew, and I got involved in several moneymaking ventures, including building and operating a Dairy Queen franchise right outside the back door to my office.

One day, while I was having lunch at the Dairy Queen with my family, just as I did every day, I saw something that floored me. A man and a woman were walking across the driveway from my company toward the Dairy Queen, and when I looked at them, I thought to myself, "Man, that guy is the spitting image of Ralph Rocky. But it can't be Ralph because he's been dead for years."

The man walked into the Dairy Queen with this woman, who was using a cane and looked as though she may have had a mild case of cerebral palsy. They ordered lunch and sat down in a booth near us. I kept glancing over at the couple as I ate but tried to return my attention to my family so as not to seem rude.

Finally, the man got up from his booth, walked over to me, and said, "I thought I would come up to see you today, Ralph."

My eyes bulged. I was in shock. I said, "You, you're— you're alive."

He said, "Yeah, well, looks like I am." Then his face twitched, just like it always used to.

"But a buddy called me and told me he read your obituary in the paper a while ago," I said.

"No, I didn't die," he said. "But I'll tell you what. My wife did. He must've seen her obituary."

I stammered. "I mean, well, that's just … your wife came to see me just before you … when you were ill and wanted me to buy your business because you were dying, and I—I …"

"Well, I survived, and she died," he said. "Isn't that incredible?"

Once I got over the shock, I left business to the others for the day and spent the rest of that afternoon with Ralph and his friend. Ralph had successfully sold his business and was retired, but he still had much to teach me.

For one thing, I was reminded again of how precious life is, and I was determined not to lose contact with him again. He was about 25 years older than I was, and I made a point to see and talk with him as often as I could, until he actually did pass away a few short years after that.

For another thing, Ralph was the person who taught me the lesson about pricing my products accurately. He said, "If you don't price fairly, you are not going to be there to help anybody else. You have to price this stuff right. You have got to be honest about your pricing, because otherwise you won't stay in business, and then you won't do anybody any good."

Ralph was also a big proponent of value and quality. The lawn mower deal we struck was a good example. The company selling the lawn mowers went out of business. Ralph and I then took the exact same parts those lawn mowers were made out of, assembled them correctly, and sold every single one of them we made.

It wasn't just the price, and it wasn't just the quality; it was the combination of the two that worked.

Ralph was a self-made man, and by his example I learned I could be a self-made man, too. I listened as he told me how he started his business by selling parts for lawn mowers out of the back of his truck; how every day he traveled around Indiana, from one lawn mower repair shop to another, to sell those parts; and how after he built some customer loyalty with that strategy, he established a mail-order business that enabled him to make sales through his catalog and then ship the products instead of hand-delivering them, thereby reducing his travel and overhead costs.

This really stuck with me. In my earlier days, I used to drive more than 50,000 miles a year to Veterans Affairs (VA) hospitals, to customers' homes, and to places where I knew people might appreciate my products. As time went on, I was able to figure out that I could have a greater reach and exposure at far less cost by advertising. That didn't mean that I completely stopped visiting places, but it did mean that a proper marketing mix required more than just one approach.

I also learned a great deal at my quality control job. Because we made automotive switches, our big customers were Ford, General Motors, and Chrysler—even Studebaker, before it went out of business. From a process perspective, my job placed me essentially at the intersection of customers and suppliers, and from that vantage point, I had free reign to observe the goings-on of business. If the auto manufacturers had problems with the assembled pieces, it was my job to figure out why there was a failure. In addition to learning a lesson about quality, I developed a keen eye that enabled me to know at a glance whether a product was made to specifications. During those days, more times than not I could challenge an engineer and be right, even if he did have his fancy instruments to work with.

Just as I am happy to call Ralph one of my mentors, I'm glad that I've been a mentor to others. One such person whom I've mentored is Mike Bruno, who started a company called Bruno Independent Living after working for me as vice president of sales in the early 1980s.

Mike moved his family to Winamac after a successful career in Wisconsin, where he and his family were originally from. Mike was a true sales professional and was instrumental in developing our dealer network and in really making our sales take off. I loved being around his energy, and we made a good team, with me developing products and him selling them. I look back at our time together with wonder—he was so driven he made me look like I was standing still.

However, after adapting to our company and to Winamac so well, his wife became homesick and said she wanted to move back to Wisconsin. Mike was in a tough spot; he loved his job and had a lot of room to grow, but he also wanted to accommodate his wife's wishes to be near her family. He opted to leave Braun and move home but not before coming to me with an offer. He wanted to start a business that would not exactly put him in competition with me but would be somewhat in the realm of what I was offering. Because our businesses had similarities, Mike needed my consent to make it happen, so we struck a deal. I gave him my blessing, and he moved back to Wisconsin to start his business.

Only a few months down the road, Mike called me and said he was having some financial difficulty. He had a shipment coming in and didn't have the money to pay for it. It was a typical cash flow problem—in fact, one that I'd faced from time to time. I thought about Mike's predicament. I knew that I could have easily bailed him out; however, I also knew if I stepped in for him, he wouldn't learn the lesson he needed to learn. So, like a father giving his son tough love, I swallowed hard and said, "Mike, here's the deal. In order for you to really ever run this business, you've got to be standing on your own two feet. You've got to be self-sufficient. If I loan you this money, you're never going to develop a relationship with a bank and be able to go forward on your own."

Mike asked, "Oh, well, how do I go about getting the money from a bank?"

I gave him a few ideas and said, "You can do this." After we hung up, I felt terrible, like I'd really let him down in his time of need. That situation was very hard, and I wondered about him often.

A few weeks went by, and I hadn't heard from him. Curiosity got the best of me, so I called him. "Hey," I said. "What's going on? Did you get your shipment in?"

I'll never forget his response. He said, "Oh, yeah, no problem. I got the shipment in, and everything is fine." He paused. "I want to thank you."

I said, "Thank me? What for? Aren't you mad at me for not loaning you the money?"

"Oh, no, no, no," he said. "Just the opposite. I went to the bank just like you said, and I got things set up. Now I have a good line of credit that I can borrow from, and it's going to work out just great."

"Good," I replied. "That makes me feel a lot better. Because I was really hurting when I hung up that phone having said no. But I didn't think I was going to be doing you a favor by telling you yes and just by writing a check to you."

He said, "And you were right. You were dead-on."

A few years went by, and we corresponded back and forth. One day he called to tell me he had won a Small Businessman of the Year award. His business had grown like crazy. He said,

"I owe this to you. You taught me, and you gave me the knowledge on how a business should and shouldn't be run. I learned a lot of what I know from watching you and listening to you. Then I just went and did exactly what I saw you doing. That's how I got the award."

I'll tell you, with all of the things I've accomplished in my life, that interaction with Mike was one of the happiest, most satisfying experiences I've ever had. He passed away a few years ago, and I miss him terribly. One thing gives me solace in his absence: just as I passed on whatever I knew to Mike, he did the same with his son, and today, the business Mike began is a thriving enterprise.

RISE ABOVE

The Braun homestead in Winamac, Indiana, where I spent much of my
childhood. I developed my mechanical abilities tinkering in the garage
and in my cousin's farm shop.

My sister, Joan, and I
celebrate our parents'
fiftieth wedding
anniversary. Since
my diagnosis of
muscular dystrophy
at the age of six, my
parents, Joseph and
Olive Braun, worked
tirelessly to make
sure I had the same
opportunities as my
peers.

RISE ABOVE

How one man's search for mobility helped the world get moving

Me as a young boy riding a motorized wagon—my first experience with a mobility vehicle—advertising a local restaurant as my father looks on.

After several attempts, including the four-wheeled "Frankenstein," I finally came up with a workable mobility solution. Orders for Tri-Wheelers soon came in from across the country.

To make the commute to my day job as a quality control manager for a nearby manufacturer a little easier, I equipped an old mail carrier Jeep with hand controls and a hydraulic tailgate lift. I could now travel completely independently.

Whether carrying me on his back or fighting the local school board for greater accessibility, my father was a constant source of support for me.

RISE ABOVE

*How one man's search for mobility
helped the world get moving*

"Corporate headquarters" of Save-A-Step Manufacturing,
in the garage behind my parents' house, circa 1970.

Save-A-Step ID tags were
placed on all Tri-Wheelers
in the late '60s.

PHONE 946-3429

Save-A-Step
Manufacturing Co.

"CUSTOM BUILT ELECTRIC WHEEL CHAIRS"

401 S. FRANKLIN ST.

WINAMAC, INDIANA   RALPH W. BRAUN

Dodge introduced the first full-sized, front engine van in 1970, and my brother-in-law and I built the first "Lift-A-Way" wheelchair lift soon after.

HIGH QUADS WILL HAVE NO TROUBLE ROLLING ON AND OFF OUR NEW FLAT PLATFORM. OUR NEW BUILT-IN SAFETY STOP GIVES COMPLETE SECURITY WHILE LEAVING THE PLATFORM COMPLETELY CLEAR.

I continued to refine the design of my lift by incorporating safety features that have become the industry standard today.

RISE ABOVE

How one man's search for mobility helped the world get moving

News of my wheelchair lift spread, and I assembled a team to help fill orders from across the nation for Lift-A-Way lifts. As demand increased, I made the difficult decision to quit my full-time job and focus on my part-time business.

In the early '70s, Save-A-Step Manufacturing moved to an old tractor dealership with 4,000 square feet and an empty lot to park the growing number of conversion orders.

Long-time employees Karl Beck (left) and Burnie Blackmon (right) demonstrate the Lift-A-Way lift and the ample headroom of the early Braun conversion vans of the '70s.

In 1977, Miss Wheelchair America, Beverly Chapman, was given a Braun conversion to use during her reign. This led to a long-standing friendship between Bev and me.

RISE ABOVE

How one man's search for mobility
helped the world get moving

Pulaski County Journal

Winamac, Ind., Wednesday, June 6, 1979

This is what it looked like Monday night as flames quickly covered the Braun Corporation

Fire almost destroys Braun Corporation

Fire badly damaged the Braun Corporation Monday night in what could be the worst fire in Winamac in five years.

Firemen received the call at approximately 11:00 p.m. from neighbors just south of the business, located at 1014 S. Monticello.

Winamac Fire Chief Ralph Galbreath, said the fire apparently started in, or near a paint storage area located at the southwest corner of the building.

"When I arrived at the scene, the only visible flames were shooting from the roof on the southwest corner," said Galbreath.

Firemen were forced to fight the fire from outside the building for the first 45 minutes as they were unable to gain entry.

At 11:45, firemen forced two rear doors open which allowed them to get closer to what Galbreath thought might be the source of the flames, the paint room.

Back-up units from the county were called in, but Winamac fire crews ran out of water at about 11:25.

Units from Star City arrived on the scene at 11:35.

Fortunately for firemen, power lines on the west side of the building were not knocked loose by flames which surrounded wires for quite some time.

The fire was finally brought under control at 12:00 midnight. The entire south end of the building, mostly offices and storage, was destroyed.

At press time, neither the exact cause of the fire, nor total extent of damages were known.

In 1979, the Braun Corporation suffered a devastating fire at its corporate headquarters. Lift production immediately resumed outside in the parking lot while damage in the manufacturing area was repaired.

chapter nine

NEITHER RAIN NOR SNOW

There's always one moment in life when the
door opens and lets the future in.

-- Graham Greene

IN THE long, hot summer of 1967, as thousands of people my age hitchhiked to San Francisco for the "Summer of Love," I rode my motorized wheelchair back and forth to work in Winamac. The difference between the "hippies" and me could not have been clearer: while they sought answers in drugs, sex, and rock and roll, I sought mine through faith and hard work. Let them go crazy, I thought; I have more important things to do—for example, providing for my family, which had grown by one, thanks to the birth of my son, Todd, in early July.

I also had a new wrinkle to contend with: the company I was working for announced it was going to build a new factory on the outskirts of town, about two miles from where I lived. That was good news to many because it was an indication the company was doing well enough to expand into a nice new facility. Employees might have to drive for two more minutes, so to them it was no big deal. To me, it was huge. Not only would I still be riding my scooter through the elements but I'd be doing it for *two miles*—each way, every day.

By this point, my scooter had a lot of mileage on it, as did I. This was not going to work for me. At the same time, with a young child and a newborn in the house, not to mention the fact I was working nights and weekends on my own business, I couldn't ask my wife to drop everything and drive me to and from work every day. That would be too much of a burden for her to bear. What was I to do?

As it often did when faced with an obstacle, my mind went into search mode.

I thought about putting to use one of the King Midget cars I used to drive as a kid, but the idea of me, a grown man, riding to work in something like that seemed ridiculous. Plus, I'd have to go back to keeping one chair at work and another at home. What's more, I'd need help transferring to both chairs once I reached them.

I wondered whether I could somehow modify my scooter, maybe by putting a top on it, but that, too, was unworkable. I'd already built one Frankenstein, and I did not want another.

I also considered getting someone else to drive me, but I ruled that out when I thought of how dependent I'd be on somebody. Wasn't my goal to be self-sufficient and in the mainstream of society? If I wouldn't ask someone in my own family, how could I ask someone outside of it?

As the months wore on and the weather got worse, I started to panic. Just when I thought all hope was lost, I got an idea: what if I had a vehicle with enough space inside so I could ride my scooter right up into it and then drive while sitting on my scooter? I couldn't use my legs, but I still had plenty of strength left in my arms to steer with. I thought if I hooked up some hand controls, I could apply the gas and brake when I wanted to; I could operate the vehicle all by myself. It seemed plausible, but with one problem: I had no idea what the vehicle might be.

I started on my quest, and before long, I felt like I was getting closer to a solution. I was focused and encouraged because I had read about a place in Indianapolis that had bought a cast-off U.S. postal vehicle at a surplus sale. I remember thinking, I've seen postal workers loading and unloading those trucks before. They're basically empty shells with a lot of room inside. What if I add some hand controls, take out the driver's seat, and come up with some kind of lift so I can get up in there with my scooter? That might work, right?

I went to Indianapolis to look at the old postal vehicle. It was a Jeep FJ-3 Fleetvan, which was a small, easily maneuvered cargo carrier built between 1961 and 1965 by Kaiser-Jeep and Willys Motors, in Toledo, Ohio. Sometimes referred to as "the Forgotten Jeep," the Fleetvan had an F-134 Hurricane engine and a Borg-Warner automatic transmission and was right-hand drive, which meant the person operating the vehicle sat on the right side instead of the left. Only 135 inches long, 90 inches high, and 65 inches wide, the Fleetvan weighed 3,000 pounds and carried a 1,000-pound payload on 80 inches of wheelbase.

The Fleetvan was similar in appearance to today's FedEx delivery trucks. In reality, it was an early minivan—and it seemed like a dream come true.

It was old, and it wasn't much more than a bucket of bolts, but it was mine.

After I bought the Fleetvan, I went with one of my uncles, Roger Freeman—who used to let me drive around the yard in the motorized wagon he built for me when I was a kid—back to Indianapolis to pick it up. We took his flatbed grain truck, put the Fleetvan on it—it was in such bad shape that it wasn't even roadworthy—and drove back to Winamac. We took it to my parents' garage, where my dad kept his Marathon truck and where I built Tri-Wheelers.

Once we got the Jeep inside, I sat and looked at it. Its floor was about 30 inches in the air, and when you're in a wheelchair, 30 inches might as well be Mount Everest. I thought, OK, that's nice—now how am I going to get in there? If I could get someone to open the door for me, put a ramp down, pick it up after I got inside, and then close the door, I could do it. But once again, that would have made me dependent on someone else, and I didn't want that.

Then I remembered a company I'd heard about in Silver Lake, Indiana, that was making a power tailgate for a pickup truck. It was a relatively new idea, and I thought I might be able to adapt that and put it on the back of my Jeep, so I called them up.

"Hi, this is Ralph Braun, and I heard about a power tailgate you're selling."

"Yeah," the bored voice on the other end said.

"I want to buy one," I continued.

He brightened a bit and asked, "What kind of pickup truck do you have?"

"I don't have a pickup truck," I said. "I've got a Jeep."

"Oh," he said, his voice dropping. "We don't have one that will fit a Jeep."

I rolled my eyes. Couldn't anyone think beyond the obvious? "Well, let's pretend I have a pickup truck and that you're going to sell me a power tailgate."

"But you don't …"

"Just bear with me," I said.

"OK, what pickup truck do you want it made to fit?" he asked.

"Pick one," I answered.

We settled on a price, and I picked it up one week later, on a Saturday. The day was brutally cold when my brother-in-law and I drove my Chevy Bel-Air station wagon the 40 miles to Silver Lake to get my power tailgate. When we arrived, one of the plant workers came out driving a forklift carrying this massive, heavy, steel tailgate-lift contraption. He stopped in front of our car and looked at us. I swallowed hard and said, "Let's put it in the back of the station wagon."

We shoveled it into the car and watched the poor Bel-Air sink low to the ground from the weight. Driving home, I coaxed the old car along and wondered what I could possibly do with the monstrosity I was now responsible for.

I find it interesting that my parents' garage, which used to be a chicken hatchery filled with incubators where thousands of lives began, gave birth to my wheelchair business. Although I didn't know it at the time, with my "new old" Jeep and this power tailgate, another new business was about to be born.

We built the first lift-enabled wheelchair van fairly quickly. As we did in the past, we started cutting steel and putting it together. We made our own brackets and mounts and turned the tailgate into a platform—it had to be enlarged so my Tri-Wheeler wouldn't roll off it—and fastened it to the back of the Jeep.

I drove my wheelchair on to the lift, rode it up to the Jeep's floor, and went in. The sliding overhead door was impossible for me to close, but at least I was inside. I had taken out the driver's seat and installed a hand-controlled power brake unit I'd bought at an old junkyard.

That was it. I finished what I set out to do.

Today, people sometimes ask me whether I remember the first time I drove my Jeep after I'd installed the lift. They ask whether I took some kind of celebratory victory lap or drove it around town to show off my creation. They wonder whether I realized then the significance of what I'd done and how it would change the future.

Here's the unvarnished truth: there was no hoopla, no champagne, no eureka moment. I was simply tired. When we finished, I backed the Jeep out of my parents' garage, drove back to my house, and went to bed. The next day, I drove the Jeep to work—another obstacle overcome.

Its back door could not close because of the lift I'd installed, so the fact my post office vehicle was said to be "weatherproofed" did not apply. Nor did it offer the highly touted "maximum driver comfort" and an "efficient heating and ventilating system." Actually, I guess you could say it did have an efficient ventilating system because the door stayed open and allowed plenty of air to rush in, whatever the weather was. It had "plenty of glass," and if I overlooked the fact the windshield wipers never worked, it did have "great visibility." With more miles on it than a rented mule, it most definitely did not "save me money—in maintenance, gas, oil, antifreeze, and spark plugs."

My Jeep served its purpose by keeping me out of the elements and making me self-sufficient. It also gave me a sense of satisfaction that I'd used my wits and creativity to solve a very big problem for myself. Finally, after driving it for a few months, I allowed myself to think, "Hey, this is a pretty slick idea." I called a man in Bloomington, Illinois, named Ray Cheever, who ran a little magazine called *Accent on Living*, in which I would later advertise. I told him what I'd done and sent him a picture of my lift-enabled postal vehicle, and he ran a story about it. It wasn't much, and I didn't get a huge response from that article, but as I drove it over the next two and a half years, I did begin to attract some attention. That is, until the good old Jeep finally gave out on me in 1970.

Once again, a door had opened and was about to let the future in.

chapter ten

SPARKS FLY

My formula for success is to rise early,
work hard, and strike oil.

-- J. Paul Getty

IN APRIL of 1970, as my Jeep was headed to the big junkyard in the sky, I moved on without a trace of sentiment. Quickly, I turned my attention to a vehicle I'd seen at the local Dodge dealer. It was called a B-van, fresh off the assembly line, and when the salesman opened the side doors and I looked inside, my eyes just about fell out of my head.

Put another way, I knew that one day sparks would be flying between us.

This new van was a big deal for two reasons. First, I had never bought a new vehicle before, so the purchase would represent a sizeable portion of my income. Second, unlike any other model on the market at that time, the van's engine was pushed forward. Because the floor was also relatively flat, once I took out the driver's seat, I'd have a clear path all the way up to the steering wheel.

To make it even more attractive, the B-van was greatly improved over its predecessor. In addition to features that increased its performance, the van was stylish, with a dashboard, trim, and comfortable seats that were as good as, if not better than, those in passenger cars. Finally, it came with power steering, power brakes, air conditioning, and a fresh-air heater and defroster.

Compared with my post office Jeep, this was like a living room. The possibilities were endless. I could take my family to church. I could go anywhere.

Even though I knew I had to have it, I was determined to play it cool in the negotiation, just like my father taught me. If I gave away too much information too early, I'd be showing my hand, like a poker player, and the salesman would have the advantage.

Slyly, I lobbed my question, "How much are you asking for this thing?" I figured "this thing" would make it seem less important to me.

The salesman smiled. "$3,200."

"I'll take it," I blurted out. The salesman kept smiling. It was only $100 less than the price of my trailer home.

As I left the dealership, my mind was wired. I could not wait for delivery. I started calling on a daily basis to ask when it would arrive. The van was made in Windsor, Ontario, and because it was a brand-new vehicle, they said I would have to wait for delivery from Canada.

That was not the answer I was looking for.

I pressed further, really becoming a pain in the neck. Finally, in August, they did something unprecedented in those days: they loaded my van on a truck by itself and drove it straight to my parents' garage from Canada.

I rubbed my hands in anticipation. It was time to start cutting steel.

The van had side doors and rear doors, and both opened on hinges, like a barn door would. I didn't take long to figure out where I'd install my lift. The rear entry was out of the question because I wanted to have seats back there so my family could ride with me—a family that now included my son, Brent, who had been born two years earlier, and my son, Drew, who was due in April of the following year.

Because I wanted the van to look good and not just take me back and forth to work, this was a much harder conversion than the Jeep. My trusty saw would have to wait until I made some drawings and figured out what to do.

One day at the factory, where I still worked full time, I was looking at the way a fork truck used hydraulics and chains to raise and lower what it was carrying. I reasoned that if I got some pieces of tubing that could slide inside each other telescopically, as well as some cylinders and a pump, I could build myself a lift that would be durable and reliable.

Back at the garage, I looked at the name on the pump from the old Jeep. It was Monarch Road Equipment, out of Grand Rapids, Michigan. After I spoke with the company on the phone, a salesman came to see me the next day. His name was John Mahan, and he would become a very important person in my life.

John was already at my parents' house when I got there after work. With no pretense of cool, I said, "I want to buy one of these pumps." We went in the garage, where he saw his company's familiar pump on the Jeep.

I told him what I had done with the Tri-Wheelers and how I started out making one for myself and then made a successful business by making them for others. I said it wasn't out of the question that the same thing could happen with lifts. I said, "If things go well, I'll probably be buying a lot more from you."

"Well, how many do you think you're going to buy?" John asked. "I need to know what kind of quantity pricing I should put you in because I need to answer to my boss as to what I sell you the first pump for."

"If you price them right, I'm guessing that I'll be able to make a bunch of these and sell them," I replied. "If you charge me too much, I won't be able to sell as many, and then I won't be able to buy as many."

He rubbed his chin and studied me. "That's an interesting approach," he said. "I've never had anybody say that to me before."

I said, "Well, that's the way I see it. If you give me the right price, every pump I buy will be from you."

After calling his boss, John gave me the same high-quantity, rock-bottom price that he gave people who built hundreds or thousands of snowplows or forklifts a year. This kind of thing didn't happen very often, if at all—especially with a big company like Monarch and a little outfit like mine, based in a garage.

We made the deal, and we both kept our word. To this day, Monarch Road Equipment has been my one and only pump supplier, and we're one of its top customers.

John became a very close mentor and friend to me and my family. My kids loved him so much they called him "Uncle John." Years later, when his wife got sick, she had one of our wheelchair vans. When John died, my youngest child, Melissa, who was born in 1975, actually wrote his obituary for the newspaper she was publishing, *The Pulaski County Journal*.

Eleven years older than me, John gave me priceless business training. He told me how tough it was going to be with me starting the business from the ground up. He said until I got some white in my hair, nobody was going to believe a word I said. Like it or not, he said, that was how it was going to be. He was right.

John's advice taught me I needed to be much more attentive, and that much more believable, with a full head of dark hair. I knew I needed to go that extra step. Of course, the fact I was in a wheelchair meant I had to overachieve to an even greater degree.

I learned from John during the rest of his life and even did more business with him after he retired from Monarch. He had moved to Ohio and started a couple of businesses of his own, one selling garbage truck parts and the other sewer cleaners. John combined them into one mail-order company and was successful with it for a few years. In 1994, when he became ill and could no longer work, I bought the business from him and moved it to Winamac. I put one of my best people in charge, Tom Bonnell, and merged it with Mobility Products and Design, another company I'd purchased that made hand controls for accelerators and brakes. Later, because it didn't fit with my company's focus, we sold the garbage truck and sewer business. Today, I still own Mobility Products and Design, and it is still run by Tom.

John taught me there are all kinds of ways to make money in this life and that while sometimes you do what you love and other times you do things purely for the financial benefit, you'd better know the difference between the two. That was the case with the sewer and garbage truck parts businesses. We built them up and then sold them off so we could get back to providing mobility solutions. I've done the same with many other successful businesses I've owned and run, including several restaurants, a trucking company, and even Braun Fiberglass, where we made portable toilets—but I always returned to the business I loved and was born to run.

However, back in 1970, acquiring other businesses was the furthest thing from my mind. In my parents' garage, I was looking into my new Dodge van with my drawings in my hand, and the thought running through my head was "Now let's build this baby."

The details of how all the pieces fit together, how all the trial and error and effort came to fruition in that first lift, are rather overwhelming to comprehend. To make a long story short, working nights and weekends, we built and installed the first lift in three weeks. As soon as I took a ride up and down on that lift, I saw that revisions needed to be made. That took another three weeks. Finally, one more revision later, we nailed it, but not without one last piece of hammering.

When I took out the driver's seat and went up under the steering wheel in my chair, I could almost reach it but not quite. I was six inches short because part of the wheel well was sticking out. I told my brother-in-law to get a sledgehammer, pull back the floor mat on my brand-spanking-new vehicle, and beat the metal down so I could get up in there. He did, and I fit right in. After we installed some tie-downs to keep my chair in place—we used something similar to gate latches—we were done.

Did I pop the champagne cork then? Did confetti fall from the sky? No. As before, I drove the new Dodge home, got some sleep, and went to work the next morning. I was excited, but I was exhausted. Working a full-time job, running my Tri-Wheeler business on the side, traveling all over the place to get parts, and being a father to a growing family had made me bone tired.

I did do one thing. A few days later, I had some pictures taken of me with my van, just as I had when I converted the Jeep, and I sent them to Ray Cheever for *Accent on Living*. He wrote up another little story about how I'd converted the new van and was driving it back and forth, and he also included the picture I'd sent him. I had no expectations of a response because the article he had done on me before hadn't generated any interest.

As soon as the article hit, my phone started ringing. People were calling from all over the place to ask how they could get a van like mine and how much it would cost them. I felt like I was answering questions on the phone all night. I couldn't take any action that night because I had to get up and go to work in the morning, but I knew I was on to something. I thought of John Mahan and said to myself, "He's going to love this."

A few days later, while I was at my quality control job, the company's personnel director came to where I was working. He told me somebody was out in the parking lot and wanted to talk to me. I thanked him and said I'd go out on my break. When I got there, sitting beside my Dodge was a brand-new Chevy van with a sliding door and Texas license plates. A kid in a wheelchair was inside the Chevy van with his mother and father. His name was Guy Buddy Davis, and when his parents saw the article in *Accent on Living*, they didn't call; they just got in their new van and drove, 19 hours straight through from Lubbock, Texas, to Winamac, Indiana.

Buddy had polio, and his parents were getting him in and out of their van by pushing him up and down 2 × 6s they were using as a makeshift ramp. They wanted to check out my van to see how it worked, so I opened it up and demonstrated it for them, letting Buddy go in and out a few times. They were amazed and wanted to learn more, so I took them over to my parents' garage and showed them around. Right away, they asked how much it was going to cost them. I told them my van was a Dodge, and it was the only one I'd converted other than my old Jeep. They had a Chevy with a sliding door and dimensions that were completely different from the Dodge's. I explained to them how the ceiling was higher, which meant the lift would need higher stanchions, and the stepwell was wider, which meant the striker plate needed to be wider. Also, the sliding door was going to be a big challenge because my van had doors that swung open.

They were rather desperate and kept asking how much it would cost. I thought about it, and after a quick calculation, I said I could do it for $795, plus $150 to install it—$945. They didn't bat an eye and asked when they could have it.

"When do you want it?" I asked.

"We want it now," said the father. "We're up here from Texas, and we want to go back with it in our van."

I said, "It's going to take me some time to put this thing together. I'm going to have to ..."

"I'll tell you what," he said, interrupting me. "We've always wanted to take a vacation in Canada. How about if we keep driving up to Canada, you tell us when we need to be back, and we'll stop back here so you can install it on our way home?"

"Wow," I said. "It could take me two weeks to get this done, maybe more."

Buddy's father said, "That's fine. We always wanted to see Canada, and we really want this for our son."

I saw how much they cared for their son and sensed how much my lift would mean to their lives. If I agreed, I'd have two weeks of long, hard nights and weekends ahead of me—but $945 would take months for me to make at my quality control job.

"You got a deal," I said.

They were elated and said they would be back in two weeks. As they backed out of the driveway and waved, I sat in my wheelchair and started mentally running through a list of parts and materials I'd need to acquire so I could do the job. I needed a pump, cylinders, some chain, and sprockets—and some people to help me. It was pretty overwhelming.

I drove home and went in the house to begin ordering parts. I had barely said hello to my wife and kids and was about to pick up the phone to make my call when the phone rang instead. Startled, I answered, "Hello? This is Ralph Braun."

A man was on the other end of the line, and he was calling from Ohio. "Hello, Ralph," he said, his words tumbling out. "I just read an article about you in *Accent on Living*. I have a Chevy van, and I want you to put one of your lifts in it. Would it be all right with you if I come over tomorrow?"

I held the phone away from my ear and looked at it, my jaw hanging open.

I could hear "Ralph? Hello, Ralph?" coming from the receiver.

The future had arrived, unannounced, with the family from Texas. Now, with this man on the phone from Ohio, the future not only had brought a friend but also was moving in—for good.

chapter eleven

CRAZY GOOD TIMES

I will prepare and someday my chance will come.
-- Abraham Lincoln

"YEAH, YEAH, I'm here," I said to the voice on the phone.

"I catch you at a bad time?" he asked.

"No, everything's fine," I said. "Where are you calling from again?"

"Ohio," he replied. "I saw you in *Accent on Living* and thought I'd come on over, tomorrow if possible."

I explained to him that it was Monday, I still had my full-time job to do all week, and I hadn't even had a chance to order the parts I needed to complete the new lift I was working on. He was insistent.

"How about if I come over on Friday night?" he asked.

"That's better," I responded. "But why do you want to come over? And why do you need to come so fast?"

"Well, I'm retired," he began. "I don't have much to do these days except look after my son. You see, my son, he … he just got back from Vietnam, and he was hurt pretty bad over there. So, you know, he's paralyzed and can't move his arms and legs. He's … he's pretty much stuck in the house, and I want to help him."

His story was heartbreaking, and I really felt for the man. Just as I had learned by making Tri-Wheelers, I was once again reminded the need for mobility does not discriminate. It doesn't care whether you're rich or poor, black or white, young or old. It doesn't care whether you're male or female, educated or uneducated, or whether you were born with a disability or acquired it by some sort of accident.

"I have a bit of a problem," I said. "I've only converted one van so far, and that's my own Dodge, the one you saw in the article. And, now, a few minutes ago, I took an order to make a lift for a family who just drove through from Texas on their way to Canada for vacation. They've got a Chevy van, so I'm going to have to go down to the Chevy dealer so I can figure out how to fit a lift for one of those vehicles. Then, when they come back through in two weeks, I have to have it ready for them."

"How about this?" he offered. "I'll come over Friday night and help you build it. Not just mine but the one for the family from Texas, too. Instead of you having to go to the Chevy dealer, you can use my Chevy van to fit it."

"Wow, that's awfully generous of you," I said.

"It's no problem for me," he said. "My son needs this real bad, and I think having this van fixed up might change his whole outlook on things."

"I imagine it might," I replied.

Then, he added, "Oh, and if you're wondering what kind of help I might be able to give you on these lifts, well, I am a retired Navy mechanic, so that ought to be of some use."

As if I needed any more convincing, that sealed the deal. He would arrive on Friday, and we'd begin work immediately. As soon as I hung up, I started calling suppliers and placing orders for double parts, enough for two Chevy vans. I also needed people to help. I couldn't simultaneously build two lifts with just this man from Ohio and my brother-in-law, and that wasn't even counting all of the Tri-Wheelers I was still making.

When I went back to work at my quality control job that day, I told my boss, Charles Stapp, what had happened and what I was going to do. I explained to him how I'd already ordered all the parts I was going to use but I also needed to hire some people on a temporary basis to help me out.

So, I hired him—my boss, that is. Not only that but also I hired two of my other coworkers.

If I had stopped to really think about what was happening, I might have become too overwhelmed to go through with it. But I didn't stop; I plowed forward. When I did, my boss and the other two guys said, "You tell us what to do, and we'll do it."

Why did they agree to help me so quickly? First, these men were my friends. Second, they were all mechanically inclined, so they knew how to do the work. Third, they had families, and they wouldn't mind making a few extra bucks. But more than anything, they wanted to see just how much I could accomplish with a little help.

People sometimes ask me how I can have a global company based in an Indiana cornfield. They ask me how I can attract and retain talent out in "the middle of nowhere." I believe it has something to do with the example of building these first lifts.

To me, having values matters. Having a good work ethic matters. Caring for your fellow man matters. These guys had all of that, and the people who work for me today do, too. What's more, I think all of that matters to our customers as well. Whether they are even consciously aware of the values, work ethic, and care that go into every single product we make, they experience those things through our quality and reliability and through the lives our mobility products help them live.

However, it's a long way from those first two lifts to today.

On the day I took those first two lift orders, I had hired my boss and two coworkers, agreed to have the customer from Ohio work with me, gotten my brother-in-law to also work on the lifts, and ordered all the parts and supplies I'd need. Then, every day after work, I drove to see Ralph Rocky, John Mahan, and all of the other suppliers so I could pick up my orders. Because these trips were so far away, each one of the suppliers had to stay open later, or even come back after their families had gone to bed, so they could get me what I needed. After I'd gotten my supplies, I'd drive back to Winamac, get some sleep, and go back to my full-time job.

Finally, at 3:30 on Friday, we started building the lifts. My hired help and I all converged on my parents' garage. When we arrived, the man from Ohio was already there, sitting in the yard beside his brand-new Chevy van. We got to work immediately, measuring the differences in dimensions between my Dodge and the Chevy and trying to figure out what it would take to make it work. Once we had the measurements in place, I told people where to make cuts, drill holes, weld things together, and so on. It was a whirlwind of activity. During that wild and crazy weekend, my entourage of worker bees was fed by my mother, who proudly welcomed them into her kitchen.

We worked as long as we could that Friday evening. At the break of dawn, we started again and worked late into the night.

During the day, we bought some fast-drying paint in cans. At the end of Saturday night, we painted the lift for the man from Ohio. I don't know how many cans we used, but it was a lot, and it was gun-metal gray. We didn't paint the other lift because that family wasn't due back from Canada for another week.

On Sunday after church, we began to install the first lift in the Chevy van. By late afternoon, we were done. I thanked the man from Ohio for his help, he paid me, and off he went, excited as any one person could be. My little gang and I nearly collapsed from exhaustion, but we were happy. I was glad to hear from the same man a few years later. He told me how the lift had indeed changed his son's outlook on life. If today I heard his son was still one of our customers, I wouldn't be a bit surprised.

The following Friday night, the Texas family came back from Canada. I drove them to the Indian Head Hotel in town, where they spent the night while we started to install their lift. The next morning, we finished installing it and brought them back from the hotel to see it. They were ecstatic. Tears were flowing everywhere, and there were hugs all around. They thanked us, paid me, and drove off to Texas with Buddy, never to use 2 × 6s again.

We then began cleaning up my parents' garage. It looked like a hurricane had blown through, with paint cans, discarded scraps of metal, and other debris covering the place. We had just made and installed two lifts in two weeks. As I looked at the scene in wonder, it was almost unbelievable.

Before I could exhale, my mother stuck her head out of the door to tell me I had a phone call. Apparently, a man had tracked me down at my parents' house, from Boston this time, to place an order for a conversion on his van. I went in the house and spoke with him on the phone. He was calling on behalf of a very wealthy lawyer, a real old-money Boston Brahmin, and he wanted me to convert his Dodge van right away. As with the other two orders, I listened as the man described how the lawyer had seen the article about me and wanted the exact same thing as I had, only with an automatic power lift and doors. He wasn't going to drive it like I did, but he just wanted to be able to press a button and have it work. The vans I had just finished converting and that we were still cleaning up from were only semiautomatic because the lift powered up and down but unfolded manually. This man from Boston wanted the whole thing.

Because I would mostly be able to copy what I'd done with my own Dodge for this Boston customer, I knew exactly what to do. However, with each lift I made a lot of improvements, and consequently, I wasn't able to save much time. Every lift was a work in progress; it was like I had a research process and a manufacturing process going all at once. As a result, the lifts were getting better each time.

With all of those variables in place, I was able to build and install the lift for the lawyer from Boston in three weeks. I never saw him because the other man drove the van out and back on his behalf, so I can only imagine what impact his new van had on him.

Like clockwork, I received another such call shortly thereafter. It was from a man in Kokomo, Indiana, who worked for a subsidiary of General Motors called ACDelco. GM had given him a new Chevy van, and he wanted to know whether I could convert it like I'd done with my Dodge. He wanted to be able to drive it and also have everything work automatically, including the sliding door. When I told him I didn't know how to make a Chevy van's door slide open and closed automatically, but I did know how to do a Dodge, I got a lesson in brand and company loyalty.

"Listen," he said. "I work for General Motors. Unless I want my head handed to me, which I don't, there is no way on God's green earth that I am going to drive a Chrysler product into a GM parking lot, get out of it, and go inside to work."

"Right, yeah," I muttered. "I see your point."

"Whatever it takes to make this van workable, do it," he said. "I don't care what it takes, and I don't care what it costs—just do it."

After six weeks of hard work and headaches, I finally converted his Chevy van. It was very expensive, but we did it, and I learned a lot in the process.

We'd converted four vans, not including my own, in about two months. I did this while working at my quality control job all day, taking calls from customers and driving to get parts and supplies all night, and building lifts and Tri-Wheelers all weekend. I was both exhausted and exhilarated, but at no time did I even entertain the thought of slowing down. In fact, I started to think about hiring a couple of full-time employees to help with the workload. Moreover, because the article about me in *Accent on Living* had generated such demand, I ran an ad in the magazine, too. I also ran an ad in *Paraplegic News*, a magazine run by an organization called Paralyzed Veterans of America.

We were riding a hurricane, and I did not want to let go.

One day, a Friday, I returned home from work and looked at the list of people who had called me that day. It was two pages long. Both of the advertisements had included my phone number, and the phone was ringing off the hook. I thought I must be some kind of master marketer. Encouraged, I would work my way down the list that night and over the next week, calling and setting up appointments, answering questions, and taking orders. Exactly one week later, on Friday, I'd come home from work to find the list had jumped back up to two pages. This was following a pattern, and I didn't understand it.

Finally, a lightbulb flipped on in my head. On Thursday evenings, NBC was running a hit crime drama TV series called *Ironside*, starring Raymond Burr. In the series, Burr played the role of Robert Ironside, a former chief of detectives for the San Francisco Police Department who had been paralyzed by a would-be assassin's bullet and, as a result, had to use a wheelchair to chase bad guys. Unwilling to give up his personal war on crime, Ironside continued his work for the police department as a "special consultant." He lived and worked in the attic of the police department headquarters. More important, in each episode, Ironside cracked his case by traveling from crime scene to crime scene in a van specially outfitted to help him get in and out in his wheelchair. Of course, Raymond Burr was not paralyzed and did not need a wheelchair except to play his role, and the van itself was merely a prop, but the point was driven home each Thursday night every time Ironside went in and out of the van. Clearly, the lengthy call list I got each Friday afternoon was the result of two things: my ads gave people the phone number, and Ironside gave them the motivation.

Who would have ever thought a famous Hollywood actor like Raymond Burr would drive sales for me, a guy in an Indiana garage? While some of it had to do with what I was offering, I also knew a lot of it had to do with timing and with being in the right place at the right time—which would play an even bigger role in the days ahead.

chapter twelve

MOMENT OF TRUTH

I want to put a ding in the universe.

-- Steve Jobs

I WORKED full time at my quality control job during the day but on nights and weekends made, sold, and installed wheelchair lifts for vans and built Tri-Wheelers.

Then it got busy.

Still working in my parents' garage, I designed two basic lift models: one called the Lifter and the other called the Lift-a-Way, for both Dodge and Chevy vans. These designs could accommodate a van whether it had sliding doors or doors that swung open—that is, until both Dodge and Chevy began offering a choice between sliding doors and swinging doors. Because each model had different dimensions, I had to design two more models. So, all in all, we ended up with four lift models. In addition, the Tri-Wheelers were still custom-made to fit each person's height, weight, and individual needs.

Things were getting a little out of control, even for a guy like me who flew by the seat of his pants. I was trying to design lift models so our manufacturing process could become more automated, but it was hard because not only was I learning as we went along, but also the van models were evolving at the same time. Although I had outsourced the building of parts for the Tri-Wheelers to people around town, I was still designing, selling, assembling, and delivering them, and I had not figured out a standardization process. What's more, we were rapidly outgrowing my parents' garage. My dad's Marathon truck had long been relegated to the outdoors, and now my business was beginning to spill outside the building, too. What was I going to do?

I got kidney stones and went into the hospital for an operation—that's what I did. It was exceedingly painful, and I went on disability for a short time. How painful was it? In 1901, a 6,700-year-old Egyptian mummy was found to still have a kidney stone in his pelvis. Legend has it that although this ancient man is long deceased, to this day, if you listen closely, you can still hear him howl in agony.

At that point, a logical person would have hunkered down and stayed in bed to get better, but that wasn't me. I was ambitious, and when I saw an opportunity, I was not going to let it slip through my fingers.

That's when I moved my business out of my parents' garage and into a vacated John Deere dealership in town. As a boy, I used to play there with my friend John Rausch, whose family owned the building and the John Deere franchise. John and I had remained good friends, and when he told me his family wasn't going to run the dealership anymore, I struck a deal with them. For $200 per month, on a month-to-month basis, I rented the 10,000-square-foot building and moved my business in. I paid for this with money I'd saved and from the cash flow I was getting from the sale of each lift and Tri-Wheeler. In addition, because I had so much space to work with, I was able to bring the manufacturing of the Tri-Wheelers back in-house, which saved me labor costs.

My grand enterprise had one welding table, a cut-off saw, and an iron worker called "the Little Scotchman." I had purchased most of this equipment from Studebaker through a surplus outfit after the car company had ceased production in 1963. To put my manufacturing operations in context, consider this: in the John Deere building, we had one welder, which cost me $800; today, we have several hundred welders at many more times the cost. We had one cut-off saw, which cost me $700; today, I have many of them. I had one iron worker, which cost me $2,500; today, we use very expensive lasers and much more advanced technology.

The good thing was I was then able to house all of that equipment in a building other than my parents' garage. The bad news was I had to house it in the John Deere building, which was filthy and leaked like a sieve. It rained more inside than it did outside. I was always concerned for whoever was working at the welding table or with any other electricity because of the water. We were constantly moving tables around to avoid new leaks.

When I finally recovered enough from my kidney stone operation, I went back to work at my quality control job. However, the pace that I'd been keeping was too much for me. I went to my boss, the same guy who had worked for me part time on the first couple of lifts, and told him I was going to have to leave my job. I had two full-time employees in my own business, Ed Heath and Larry Rausch, my friend John's brother, and I was going to go join them. I reasoned that my business was growing to the point that I thought I could make it on my own.

In response, my boss said, "Well, would it help if we put you on the second shift? That way, you can work all day long at your business and then come in here and work all night long."

Nice guy, right? Then, he added, "If you're lucky, you can get five minutes of sleep before you get up and go to your business in the morning."

He was kidding about the sleep, but that is what he wanted me to do. He had been very good to me, a real friend who had helped me in those initial days with my business. I felt I owed it to him to do what he had in mind. Plus, I also figured it could all work out as he'd described, and of course the paycheck wouldn't hurt. So I said yes.

I kept up this new grueling schedule for about three or four months, until, finally, I'd had enough. After 10 years of simultaneously building my own business while working full time at my quality control job, I made the decision to go completely out on my own. When I told my boss, he gave me a six-month leave of absence, unpaid, so I could see whether my plan would succeed. He told me that if it didn't work out, I could come back and retain the seniority I'd built over the past 10 years. It was a very generous offer, and I accepted.

That was a big moment of truth for me. Leaving the security of a steady paycheck to strike out on my own, with a new product in an undeveloped market, was going to be really risky. I had no financial backing and no backlog of orders that would give me the necessary confidence. Yet, I was very confident it would work. In fact, I was sure of it. Perhaps it was the typical cockiness and belief of entrepreneurs everywhere, but it was exactly what I believed.

Looking back, I can see how truly well prepared I was for that moment of truth. I had spent 10 years simultaneously building my business and working full time as a quality control inspector. The quality control job had honed my eye to the degree that I could look at a piece of metal and know its dimensions with as much accuracy as a trained engineer. It taught me how all of the elements of a business work together in an ecosystem of supply chain, sales, customer service, engineering, manufacturing, accounting, marketing, and so on. It taught me about business ethics and values and about what to do and what not to do. Working approximately 40 hours per week for 10 years had given me about 20,000 hours of experience. I thought of author and "pop sociologist" Malcolm Gladwell's observation that a person becomes an expert at something after 10,000 hours; that meant I'd achieved my expertise five years earlier, and that wasn't even counting the similar amount of hours I'd put into my own business. I was ready.

One of the first things I needed to do was incorporate my business as The Braun Corporation. I had been calling it Save-a-Step Manufacturing Company when I was making just Tri-Wheelers, but now it was growing to be a much different type of company. So in the early part of 1973, I hired Burnie Blackmon on a part-time basis to do the accounting necessary to incorporate my business. I had met Burnie when he came to take a look at my wheelchair vans, and I was impressed with him. He had owned a trucking business with his father, and because of a swimming accident 13 years earlier, he was in a wheelchair like I was. Because I had also hired another brother-in-law of mine named Buster Jensen, Burnie was employee number four, not counting me. We were doing well.

The John Deere building, however, was not doing so well. It had plenty of space, but so did the great outdoors, and with all of the holes in that building, we might as well have been outside. With that faulty work environment weighing heavily on me, I made another big decision: I would buy a building of my own and move my operations there.

The building I wanted to buy was being used by Case International Harvester to sell farm tractors. I'd heard they were vacating the building, so I knew it was going to be empty. I also knew I needed to move fast because other people wanted the building, too. It was 4,000 square feet and had an empty lot next to it where I could park customers' vans that I was going to convert. It had only one small office, but I figured I could stuff us in there until we grew enough to get some bigger space. The price was going to be $25,000, which was a fortune to me—a couple of years earlier, I had bought my van for $3,200 and thought that was a huge amount. The big question for me was the money. Where was I going to get it?

Like many small-business owners, I went to the bank: First Union and Trust Company, the only bank in town. When I told John Mahan I was going to secure financing so I could buy the Case building, he warned me they probably wouldn't give me the money, but I might as well try anyway.

I made an appointment with the president, Ralph E. Horner, a white-haired, 60-year-old man in a dark pinstriped three-piece suit. He was known around town as a real Ebenezer Scrooge, a crotchety guy who was stingy with both the bank's money and his own. He was part of the Winamac old-boy network, or "town fathers," as we used to call them, and they detested the idea of development that didn't have to do with farming. Only four other businesses in town were not farm related, and people like Ralph Horner resented every one of them. There I was, trying to get a loan to buy a building that used to have an agricultural business and turn around and use it for a non-farm-related business.

With that as a backdrop, I went to the bank. Ed Heath pushed me in a manual wheelchair because there were no curb cuts and no ramps, which meant I wouldn't be able to get into the building otherwise. As I waited for Ralph Horner, I did not feel confident. Sitting in a manual wheelchair and having to rely on someone to push me around put me in an unfavorable negotiating position.

You might think I went to that meeting with my business plan in hand, with costs, sales projections, profit, market share, and everything else that would help me make my case. I did not. I had the information, but it was all in my head. In my naiveté, I thought my word and my honor were enough for the bank to give me a loan. I learned, very rapidly, that the financial world didn't operate that way.

Mr. Horner dispensed with any pleasantries and got right down to business. "What's your asset value?" he asked.

"Well, I have a van that's fully paid for," I replied. "It's 3,000 bucks worth. I have equity in my house, which I paid $9,000 for."

"Nine thousand dollars is how much you bought the house for," he growled. "How much equity do you have?"

"I have a 33-year mortgage, and I'm paying $50 a month," I said. "So I ..."

He huffed dismissively. "Why did you quit your full-time job?"

"I started this business building Tri-Wheelers 10 years ago," I said, "and now it's grown to include these lifts, and it's getting pretty big."

"But nobody's ever done this before!" he barked.

"Well, no," I said. "You're right. I'm the first one."

"What makes you think you can do it?" he asked.

"Well, I've been doing it for 10 years already with the Tri-Wheelers and a couple more years with the lifts, and now ..."

"What happens when you sell to everyone who needs one of these contraptions?" he sneered. "What happens when you don't have any more business?"

"If that happens, then I guess I'll go back to work at my quality control job," I replied. It seemed like an honest, sensible answer.

He frowned and looked at me condescendingly. "You should have stayed at your job. Listen, you might as well save me the headache and go back there, because there's no way I'm giving you a loan."

I left there with my tail between my legs, but I learned an important lesson: you're never as good at winging it as you think you will be.

I may have been shot down on my first attempt, but I wasn't going to let one "no" get in the way of what I wanted to accomplish. That didn't mean I was going to wait and get my information together so I could approach other banks; I assumed I'd run into the same negativity there, too, no matter how well I prepared, and I was a man in a hurry. Instead, I went back to the owner of the Case building, Dick Fahler, and tried to work out a different kind of deal.

Dick was known as a shark that preyed on the weak, on people who needed financing but couldn't get it through other means. Like a real shark in the ocean, if blood was in the water, he was there. In this case, the blood in the water was mine, because he knew I wanted the building and had gotten turned down at the bank—in a small town, everyone knows your business. People in town warned me about him, but I didn't feel like I had much of a choice because I needed to get out of the John Deere building.

I asked Dick whether we could work out a rent-to-buy situation, but he had something different in mind. He wanted to give me financing in exchange for part ownership of my company. In other words, he would hold the mortgage as a land contract in exchange for taking an equity stake in my business. I said no—but I thought it was interesting that the bank had just determined I wasn't a good investment, by turning me down for a loan, but here was this guy wanting to own part of my company. Then I remembered he was a shark, and that's what sharks do: they make the terms so favorable to them that they can't lose. For instance, I don't remember what the interest rate was, but I know it was sky-high. In addition, part of the agreement stated that if I defaulted on my payments, he would get the building back. That way, he could get money from me for as long as it took for me to default on my loan—and then get the building back. He figured that would probably happen in two years at most.

I felt confident we would succeed and said I'd agree to his terms if he put in a clause that gave me the option of paying on an accelerated schedule without any early-repayment penalty. He chuckled and agreed to what seemed to him like an absurdity because he thought I'd never make the payments, let alone accelerated payments. Other people in town felt the same way about my prospects and were mad at Dick because they thought he took advantage of me. One other man in town, George Zahrt, had wanted the building for himself and was willing to pay cash but at a lesser amount than I was willing to pay. Besides, Dick wanted to bleed me for a while first. When George heard I got the building, he said, "Well, that's all right. Those boys over there in the wheelchairs won't last long, anyway. I'll probably get the building at a better price later on."

By "the boys in the wheelchairs" he meant Burnie and me. To make a long story short, we moved into the Case building on June 1, 1973, and paid off the loan in record time. When Burnie handed Dick the payoff check, Dick mumbled some indistinguishable words and then said, "I thought I was going to get this building back!" He didn't say congratulations, and we didn't say "I told you so" because we knew in our hearts that, once again, we had confounded the critics and shocked the skeptics—and we were just getting started.

chapter thirteen

READY, WILLING, AND ABLE

The two most important requirements for major success are: first, being in the right place at the right time, and second, doing something about it.

-- Ray Kroc

IN THE mid-1970s, our business experienced dramatic growth, largely as the result of two converging circumstances: the ending of the Vietnam War and our nation's response to the special needs of the veterans returning from the war.

However, Vietnam was not the sole reason for our success during this period.

Although our business "benefited" from the events surrounding Vietnam, when opportunity came our way, we were ready, with the right technology, the right products, the right positioning, and the right people. We could just as easily have failed as succeeded. However, if we had failed, thousands of customers would not have had access to our products and would have been unable to live their lives the way they wanted to.

Let me try to put this in perspective. From 1961 to 1975, more than 6 million Vietnam veterans left the military and entered civilian life. Throughout history, veterans have returned from wars to enter society, but Vietnam was different. As a result of improvements made in evacuation and medicine during the Vietnam era, a larger percentage of veterans who may have died in prior wars survived and came home disabled. In total, by 1972, 308,000 veterans were disabled as a result of their military service.

These veterans also faced another kind of circumstance different from that of earlier soldiers. Because Vietnam veterans were going straight from the battlefields to their communities, in addition to having obvious physical injuries, they were more susceptible to psychological wounds. Combined with the antiwar sentiment they faced when they returned to the United States, Vietnam veterans had an extremely hard time adjusting to living as civilians.

As if all of this weren't bad enough, when our soldiers came back from Vietnam, they returned to find a political scandal and the country's economy in a deep recession, with inflation soaring, energy markets in turmoil, and prospects for employment dim at best.

These challenges made life increasingly difficult for Vietnam veterans, and for those who had given so much for our country, much was required. After all, as George Washington once said, "The true measure of a nation is how it treats its veterans." What's more, these veterans were also more vocal—and more effective— about getting their needs met than were veterans of earlier generations. With all of that in mind, the U.S. Congress responded with several initiatives designed to alleviate veterans' struggles and reward them for their sacrifice.

For one thing, to become fully integrated into society, these soldiers needed to have access to education. Like they did with the

GI Bill, Congress passed the Veterans Readjustment Act of 1966, which gave veterans access to the same kind of educational benefits that veterans received after earlier wars. By 1980, this legislation had trained 76 percent of those eligible, which amounted to 5.5 million veterans.

Because of the extenuating circumstances facing Vietnam veterans, many were more isolated than their predecessors, especially those who had been recently discharged. As a result, these service members were harder to find, and making them aware of the programs developed to help them was difficult. To spread the word, assistance centers were created in 21 cities, and in 1967, a field office was established in Long Binh, Vietnam, to assist soldiers even before they returned to civilian life.

In addition to educational assistance and outreach programs, Vietnam veterans also received life insurance, home loan guarantees, job training, access to treatment centers, disability payments, pension payments, and more. The number of veterans eligible to receive pensions increased exponentially between 1960 and 1978. World War II veterans were reaching age 65, when veterans were presumed qualified as totally disabled by virtue of their age alone. As a result, disability pension payments increased, from $80 million in 1960 to $1.24 billion in 1978. The number of cases jumped from 89,526 in 1960 to 691,045 in 1978. The population was becoming older and more disabled, a point supported by the following fact: 32 separate legislative acts benefiting disabled people were enacted between 1973 and 1974, the 93rd Congress.

In terms of our business, all of these Vietnam-era developments drove demand for our products. Why? Simply put, the number of disabled people in the country was larger than ever before. Not only that but these people were becoming educated and were getting job training, and they were motivated to rise above their challenges and live in the mainstream of society. They needed our products, and they wanted them. The question was, How could they afford them?

The answer came, at least in part, when the VA changed the guidelines by which veterans could qualify for financial assistance to purchase products such as ours, which they referred to as "automobile and special adaptive equipment grants." Instead of providing benefits only to those injured in combat while serving in Vietnam, the VA said that all U.S. military veterans alive, regardless of where in the world they served or whether they fought in combat, were eligible to receive financial assistance so they could purchase and adapt our products.

This opened the floodgates because people needed our products more than ever, and with the VA's help, they now had the funding to purchase them. It was also retroactive. Theoretically, this meant that someone who had served in the Civil War—if that person were still alive—could receive a grant to buy our products.

If you think that's overstating it, consider this. The country's tradition of caring for veterans, spouses, survivors, and dependents is long lasting. For example, the last dependent of a Revolutionary War veteran died in 1911; in May 2006, three children of Civil War veterans were still drawing VA benefits.

Of the 24.3 million veterans alive at the start of 2006, nearly three-quarters served during a war or an official period of conflict. About a quarter of the nation's population, approximately 63 million people, is potentially eligible for VA benefits and services because they are veterans, family members, or survivors of veterans.

In the 1970s, those people were our customers, and they came to us in droves—not only the disabled but also their able-bodied family members. Once they had a disabled family member in a wheelchair, they took a totally different attitude. For example, many people, even today, say they never dreamed a company like ours was in existence until they had a child or a sibling or a parent who had become disabled. Family members learn a new life along with the person who's actually disabled; they are met with and must overcome new challenges each day right along with them.

Another reason for our rapid growth was word of mouth, which spread like wildfire and in many different directions. This continues today. People hear about us and tell all of their friends and family, then their friends and family tell their contacts, and so it goes. The most exciting aspect of this is when that word of mouth comes back to us, particularly through our dealer network. When someone in a wheelchair, or one of his or her family members, talks to one of our dealers, we become both the educator and the educated. We learn from our customers as much as we teach them. This improves our products and builds enduring relationships.

Another aspect of our story in the 1970s is this: although we benefited from legislation that was favorable to our business, we also drove—even forced—that legislation by providing an entirely new generation with the means to be mobile. Until we came along with our mobility products, many disabled people stayed indoors and kept their disabilities hidden. When they ventured out into the public eye, society was not used to seeing them out and about and didn't know how to respond. For example, when people in wheelchairs became visible, many onlookers assumed they were less intelligent or they didn't work or have careers. With our Tri-Wheelers and vans, disabled people began going everywhere, just because they felt like it. No longer did they have to plan a week in advance before they left the house; they just went. Once they were out in public, they were like anyone else. The truth is being disabled didn't change their perspective; it changed everyone else's. As disabled individuals, they had new challenges to deal with, but their hopes and dreams and fears were the same as they always were.

I'd like to believe we helped change society's attitudes through our advocacy. By advocacy, I don't mean being militant, which some disabled people became. That was not my style and never will be. I feel that I can be more productive offering opportunity rather than threats. To each his or her own, I guess.

In my case, that meant getting out and spreading the word. I put our company in the spotlight through ads and articles, yes, but just as important, I went to events and talked about what was possible. I often went with my colleague Burnie Blackmon, one of the "boys in the wheelchairs" I mentioned earlier. I remember going to nursing schools to give speeches, and it was quite enlightening. Nursing students had no idea, in those days, what it was like to be a nurse for a disabled person. They were taught how to care for someone who came into the hospital who was sick. Caring for someone who not only was sick but also had a disability was not in their repertoire. To confuse matters more, the disability had nothing do with the current visit to the hospital and everything to do with the way they had to be treated in the hospital. Were the nurses our customers? Maybe they were; maybe they weren't. They were definitely people who influenced the purchase of our products, so they were an important group to us.

It was the same thing with other groups, such as the Paralyzed Veterans of America and the National Spinal Cord Injury Association. I often spoke at conventions run by both groups and again became both the educator and the educated. So, too, did others who spoke on our behalf, such as Miss Wheelchair America, Beverly Chapman, and Jim Pauley, one of my first Tri-Wheeler customers, who said one of the most memorable lines I've ever heard. While speaking to a church group one day, as he was encouraging them to make the church wheelchair accessible, he asked, pointedly, "Does God love people who can walk better than he loves people in wheelchairs?" It is a great line, to be sure, and it aptly illustrates the passion that people have for mobility.

The ending of the Vietnam War, societal shifts in attitude, favorable legislation, and our products, technology, positioning, people, and advocacy all resulted in considerable growth. Within months of buying the Case building, which had 4,000 square feet and a parking lot, I had to put on another 6,000 square feet and then buy more property to increase the parking space. This pace of expansion continued throughout the 1970s. With each instance, the parking space was just as important as the building space. Customer vans were coming in from all over the country, night and day, and we needed somewhere to put them before they were converted with our lifts.

I was no longer "merely" an entrepreneur, but I still had that entrepreneurial itch. The question was, how was I going to scratch it?

chapter fourteen

PIONEER SPIRIT

I tried being reasonable. I didn't like it.

-- Clint Eastwood

I BELIEVE within every heart a pioneering spirit can be found: a desire to break new ground and plant seeds where there were none, to discover new things and venture forward to places we've never been, to take risks and stick our heads out of our caves—even if we get burned once in a while or run over. If it weren't so, we would never have invented fire or the wheel.

In my case, without a pioneering spirit, I would have accepted my prognosis and never left the house. I certainly never would have created my business and then continued to build it over the years. The bottom line was that no matter how big we were getting, I still loved to cut a deal, create something out of nothing, and get the most out of what I had. I still do. You see, I don't smoke or drink, play golf or tennis, or engage in a lot of other hobbies. My hobby is starting and running businesses. I love the art and science of it, and no matter how much I grow any business, I'm always looking for something else.

I inherited the entrepreneurial bug from my parents, and I'm happy to say I've passed it on to my five children. Like any parent, I never miss an opportunity to brag about my kids, so here goes: Cherie, my oldest, is trained as a travel agent but has taken on the hardest career path there is—soccer mom. Next is Todd, who, as I mentioned before, started a successful NASCAR racing team. My middle child, Brent, runs a company that manufactures seats for buses. Drew, the artistic one, channels his creative talents into a custom glass countertop and glass art business. Melissa, my youngest, is following a more unorthodox path. A mother of four, she still finds time to run an alpaca breeding farm. On a typical day, you'll find her giving shots or scooping poo, all while planning a restaurant and gift shop at the farm. Like me, they're always up for a new challenge.

I was looking for a new challenge myself back in the mid-1970s, and the answer came in the form of fiberglass. Here's the story. One day, I was looking through a magazine when I saw an ambulance with a fiberglass top for sale. We were converting a lot of vans at that time and putting 24-inch camper tops on some of them because, from floor to ceiling, there wasn't enough room for some people to go in and out unless they had extra space above their heads. When I saw the ambulance top, which was only 12 inches high, it seemed like a good thing to try on our vans. For one thing, it would be smaller and more attractive. For another, because of its smaller size, it would be much more practical in lowering the wind resistance and also decreasing the material costs.

I called the ambulance company and said, "I want to buy one of your tops."

"We don't sell tops," he said. "You have to buy a whole ambulance."

"I don't need a whole ambulance," I said. "I'm in a wheel-chair, and I need an extension for my van so I don't have to duck my head when I go in and out."

He said, "We don't sell parts unless it's for an ambulance that's been wrecked."

"OK," I said. "What if I did have an ambulance that had been in a wreck? And then that ambulance needed a new top. How much would it cost?"

"That would be $300," he said. "But you understand, I ..."

"How about if I call my van an ambulance?" I asked. "Can I buy one then?"

"I don't know ..." he said, hesitantly. I sensed he was wavering.

"Let's try this," I offered. "How about I send you a check for $300, and we'll figure out how I can come get one. How does that sound?"

He considered this for a minute, and I waited. Finally, he said, "You send me the check, and when it clears the bank, I'll call you and tell you to send somebody to pick it up. Since I don't want to get in trouble for selling you the top, I'll meet you on Sunday evening, and you can pick it up."

The following week, I sent one of my guys with a truck to pick it up. When he returned and we unloaded it on the shop floor, I said to my guys, "This is just what we need for our customers." Instinctively, I knew it was going to work.

I had some experience with fiberglass because a few years earlier I had begun making fiberglass shells to dress up our Tri-Wheelers. At this point, I had only this one fiberglass top, and I knew I needed more of them. How was I going to buy them?

I found someone in Rochester, Indiana, who was making fiberglass showers and bathtubs for the recreational vehicle (RV) industry. His name was Bill Adams, and I asked him to come look at my fiberglass top and see whether he had any ideas. Bill said he could make a mold and parts for me for less than it cost me to buy the ambulance top. On the spot, I placed an order for a half-dozen, plus the mold, which would enable him to continually make more.

Bill started making fiberglass tops for my vans, which I called "Wheelchair Traveler," and they sold like crazy. I trusted my gut, and it proved to be right. The tops were just what we needed, but they also paved the way for future advances in engineering and product design.

However, my tops were about to hit bottom, because trouble was on its way in the form of an oil embargo, which was hitting the RV industry hard. Today, Elkhart, Indiana, is all over the news because a lot of RVs are built there, and with the country in a current economic decline, Elkhart has had it rough. In the 1970s, the embargo did the same thing, because fiberglass resin is made out of oil. Consequently, sales of RVs plummeted and with it went demand for showers, tubs, and other items Bill was making out of fiberglass. Bill, like other fiberglass makers, had reached a certain allocation of fiberglass resin to make his products, but without enough demand, much of that allocation was going unused, and he was losing a lot of money.

Bill's business partner was on the verge of shutting down the business, and Bill came to let me know. He didn't have the where-withal to buy his partner out, so that looked like the end of the line for him and the fiberglass business. This was going to cause a real problem for me, because he was making van tops and Tri-Wheeler shells every day for me, and I could not lose my supplier.

To solve my problem, I bought the business from Bill and his partner, including their equipment and, most important, their allocation of oil-based resin. I then hired Bill to build my fiberglass tops and shells in a building I owned in Winamac that had been, at various points, a water ski factory and a chicken hatchery. Now I had my supply, but I was up against the same issue Bill and his partner had faced: too much allocation for too little demand. Because I was using only 5 percent of my newfound allocation, I began to look for new ways I could make up the remaining 95 percent.

Enter "Big John," my portable fiberglass toilet business.

Believe me, I've heard all the jokes about how making portable toilets was a "waste" of my money and a "stinky" business to be in. However, my thinking had some logic to it, and the business actually turned out to be quite successful.

Bill's former fiberglass partner had also owned a road construction business. Because his crews often worked in areas with no bathroom facilities, he provided them with portable toilets on the job sites. To save money by not always having to rent the toilets, Bill made him a mold so he could build his own. We still had the mold, so Bill and I decided to see whether we could put it to use.

We built two portable toilets and called them Big Johns. Bill put them in the back of his pickup truck and drove to some construction sites to see whether he could sell them. We quickly realized our "go-to-market strategy" was flawed because the people on the construction sites did not want to have to deal with cleaning and storing our Big Johns.

To improve our strategy, we joined an association of "honey dippers," an ironic nickname for people who clean out septic tanks for farmers. Their real name was the Portable Sanitation

Association, and when we took our Big Johns to their San Diego convention, we swept the market.

Many competitors were making their portable toilets out of wood. In addition to being too heavy, let's just say splinters were a problem. The unquestioned market leader, however, was a company called Virginia Fiberglass, but its product could not stand up to ours because it was much smaller and was not made as well as ours. This soon became apparent during Virginia Fiberglass's product demonstration, when the booth attendant used his cowboy boots to kick the portable toilet he was promoting to show how strong it was and put his foot through the side. He tried to talk his way out of it and even attempted to cover up the hole with some paper and tape, but the damage was done.

Our Big Johns were indestructible. They were 7½ feet tall and 4 feet by 4 feet, weighed 175 pounds, and were cream colored, with one exception—during the country's bicentennial celebration, we painted some of our Big Johns red, white, and blue.

By the end of the San Diego convention, we sold 600 Big Johns at $375 each. Within a month, we were shipping tractor trailers filled with 22 Big Johns each week to customers all over the country. Another month later, we were shipping a tractor trailer filled with Big Johns every single day. We supplied all of the portable toilets for the building of Disney's new Epcot theme park and also for the Pope's visits to Chicago and Minneapolis. Soon, I had to put up more buildings just to keep up with demand.

The portable toilet business could have gone on indefinitely, but once the oil embargo had been lifted and there was plenty of fiberglass to go around, I did not need to have so much capacity. All I really wanted was to ensure my supply for fiberglass tops and Tri-Wheelers. So in the late 1980s, I sold the fiberglass business to Bill, who continued to build my fiberglass tops and Tri-Wheeler shells for many years.

I'd gotten everything I'd wanted out of the fiberglass business: I'd ensured my supply of fiberglass, leveraged my investment to build a business, and then sold it for a fair return.

But back in the '70s, despite the fact my van and lift business was booming, I was restless. Even though I'd just started in fiberglass, I was looking for another opportunity.

One came in the form of a Snap-On tool truck—not the truck but the man driving it, Jim McDaniels, who was a Snap-On salesman. Jim had been coming around the shop and selling tools to my employees during working hours, but he wasn't happy in his job and really wanted to try something else. Part of the reason he wasn't happy was that guys like me were always telling him to get lost when he came around and tried to sell his tools.

After Jim and I had become friends, we were having lunch one day at a drive-in ice cream shop in a nearby town, North Judson. While we ate, I told him I'd always wanted to have a fast-food franchise in Winamac. To my amazement, he said he wanted out of the Snap-On business and a fast-food franchise was one of the things he would consider. We agreed that a Dairy Queen would fit well in our town, and just like that, we went to go look at one in a nearby town. After talking to the manager and getting some contact information for Dairy Queen's home office in Minneapolis, we drove back to Winamac, where I called and made an appointment for someone to come and talk to us.

A few days later, a representative from Dairy Queen came to my office to discuss the possibilities of opening a franchise. He said he needed to do a survey to see whether Winamac could support one of their restaurants. In other words, he had to determine whether Winamac had the kind of traffic that would enable a Dairy Queen to succeed. Jim and I looked at each other and thought, "We're going to get turned down now. Oh, well, it was a nice thought."

The Dairy Queen representative was a young kid and said he would do the survey himself. He would send it to the home office, and then they would contact us to let us know whether the survey came back positive. With that, he drove across the street and parked his car—and waited. He sat there for about half an hour while he counted cars.

Luckily, it was about 3:30 in the afternoon. This meant that my former employer and the other businesses in town were just finishing the first shift, so a steady stream of cars was flowing directly past where this young Dairy Queen representative sat. Finally, he drove away. One week later, we got a call from Minneapolis; for $15,000, we could have our franchise. Jim and I each put up $7,500, and we were in business.

Of course, we needed a building. For that, I called my friend Monty Williams, the man who had been building all of the structures I was constantly growing out of. Monty was somewhat of a renegade, like me, so although he knew nothing about building a Dairy Queen, he was willing to take a shot, provided he could put up the shell—someone else would have to do the interior. Because it was summer, for the interior I got Jerry Jones, a local industrial arts schoolteacher who had taught my kids and who I knew to be the best craftsman in town. Once Monty and Jerry were through with their work, we had our grand opening.

Our Dairy Queen was a huge success. Everyone in Winamac seemed to eat there, and on hot summer nights, it was the place to go. But it was more than that: my friend Jim was making a good living from it, we were employing high school kids and other people who needed jobs, and it felt good to have my town thought of like other towns. Not only was I moving up in the world but I was helping my town do the same. Today, Jim and I are still the best of friends. We go to NASCAR races in my motor home and fly radio-controlled planes together. Jerry Jones's son, Tom, works for us at Braun, and Jerry's wife, Connie, retired from the company a few years ago.

By the end of the 1970s, my pioneering spirit had served me well. What had begun with Tri-Wheelers had grown into a very successful business that also included wheelchair vans and lifts— a market we created. As a result, I told myself that with more hard work, innovation, and preparation, nothing could stop me from building the company of my dreams.

I spoke too soon.

chapter fifteen

THE FIRE

*The test of success is not what you do when
you are on top. Success is how high you bounce
when you hit bottom.*

-- George Patton

AT APPROXIMATELY 11 p.m. on June 4, 1979, our company caught fire.

I was in Seminole, Florida, when I got the call from my friend in Winamac, Jim McDaniels, who had just closed and locked the Dairy Queen, which was next door to our company building. As he shouted into the phone, I could hear sirens wailing, horns blasting, and people yelling in the background. Over the next couple of hours, his play-by-play would come fast, in short bursts, through a series of phone calls.

The fire department had been called and was on the scene. Flames were shooting 20 to 30 feet into the air. It was intensely hot, and smoke was everywhere. On the west side of the building, flames were threatening to bring the power lines down. Firemen were wearing air masks and trying to break into the locked building. They had risen high above the building in the town utility's "cherry picker" to shoot water down on the fire. Truckers from as far away as Royal Center, 15 miles to the south, said they could see the flames. At 11:25 p.m., although backup units from around the county had been called in, the Winamac Fire Department said they were out of water. By 11:35 p.m., the Star City–Van Buren Township Fire Department arrived with reinforcements. About 10 minutes later, firemen were able to get into the building by forcing two rear doors open, one by using a truck to knock down a door, the other by using an axe. They were going to the paint room, where Winamac Fire Chief Ralph Galbreath thought the fire might have started.

None of our 45 Winamac-based employees appeared to be in the building, though our company controller, Bill Roth, was on the scene, as well as Jeff Hermanson, another employee who lived two blocks away and ran to the fire in his shorts, T-shirt, and bare feet. No firefighters and no employees had been hurt, but emergency medical technicians from Ross Ambulance were also there, just in case. My father was on-site, God love him, asking the firemen whether it was really necessary that they use their axes on the door because, well, the door cost good money.

The fire was the worst anyone in Winamac could remember. While there's never a good time for a fire, the timing for this fire was particularly bad. A piece of legislation had just been passed stipulating that every school in America needed to provide accessibility for disabled students. Because it was June and school started in September, we were right in the middle of outfitting buses and paratransit vehicles all over the country. Our customers were counting on us, and we absolutely could not afford to have a work stoppage.

Unfortunately, the fire raged on, ignoring our concerns.

In between phone calls with Jim, I chartered a private Learjet to take our family back to Indiana. Because the charter company had to file a flight plan, put together a crew, and get a plane ready, I had to wait for hours before I could depart from Clearwater Airport.

Ironically, as the minutes flew by, time seemed to hang in suspended animation. I could hear myself breathe, even hear myself think. It was torture.

For some reason, I can remember watching *The Tonight Show* on television that evening before the phone call. Beverly Sills, an opera singer who had just been named director of the New York City Opera, was the guest host.

Now that I think about it, the fact that an opera singer was hosting *The Tonight Show* was fitting, since the fire was surely dramatic. I never was much of an opera fan, but if there were ever any question about my preference for that type of music, the night of the fire sealed it for me once and for all.

Finally, sometime after midnight and well before we took off from Florida, the fire was brought under control. The entire south end of the building, where the offices and storage were located, was destroyed. The rest of the building had suffered severe smoke damage but looked salvageable. The 10 vans parked inside the building were also damaged but apparently not beyond repair.

There was hope.

A few hours later, just as the sun rose on the horizon, our chartered jet touched down in Valparaiso, Indiana. Jeff Hermanson had driven to the airport to pick us up and took me to see the damage at our facility. He had been at the scene of the fire all night and was shaken and covered in ashes. The van he was driving was also covered in soot.

When we arrived at our building, I experienced a small miracle.

Soaking wet fire-retardant insulation from the ceiling had fallen on the desks below, protecting many of our records. Although it was too soon to determine whether any records had been destroyed, many important documents seemed to have been saved. In addition, because the fire had occurred primarily where the offices and storage space were located, the damage to the manufacturing end of the facility was mainly from smoke, heat, and ash; for the most part, it could be cleaned up. Still, the building was uninhabitable in the short term, and we had to figure out what to do next.

To get a bird's-eye view of the damage, my building contractor, Monty Williams, took me up in a small propeller plane and we flew over the scene. Perhaps it was because of my usual optimism in the face of obstacles, but I remember thinking we would overcome this challenge. I also remember having gallows humor and thinking, "I'd feel a lot safer down there in that smoldering building than up here in this little propeller plane."

Back on the ground, we cobbled together a place to work. For our office space, we rented a nearby filling station for 90 days and a couple of trailers for two years. Our payroll person sat writing checks at a folding card table under a tree. Office furniture and records were removed from the building and put on the front lawn. We sent most of our manufacturing employees home when they came in on Tuesday morning but told them to come back at noon the next day. Because the manufacturing portion of the complex did not appear to have direct fire damage, production schedules would not be affected that much, once we cleaned up the space with a lot of elbow grease, power-washing, and paint. In addition, we brought a few machines outside, put them on a concrete slab under a tent, hooked up some electricity, and continued working during the cleanup.

We were back in business within a few days.

In retrospect, we could have been buried by the fire's destruction. A lesser company might have succumbed to its fate. But in making the best of a bad situation, we actually forged a new and even more successful path.

Why were we able to do that? Two words: "determination" and "focus."

The determination was the easy part. Personally, I'd had a lifetime of people telling me I couldn't do things. From the doctor who said I wouldn't survive, to the school administrator who said I might as well stay home, to the man who thought "those boys in the wheelchairs" would fail, I had plenty of reasons to be motivated. The last thing I was going to do was let any of them have the satisfaction of seeing me fail, even if it was because of an unforeseen disaster that was out of my control.

What about our employees? How did they respond? Well, I've mentioned the efforts of Jeff Hermanson during the fire and its aftermath, but he would be the first person to tell you the entire company acted with the same sense of urgency. Our employees were so convinced of our survival, they actually competed against each other to see who could get more work done. In those days, we did not have an assembly line, so individuals worked side by side performing every single step of the lift-making process. They could look to their left and right and see how their "competition" was doing. To them, our company's future was in their hands, and there was much they wanted to do. It's not like they didn't have other options; several other places in Winamac paid equally well.

To reward them for their efforts during this period and to activate a long-term retention strategy, we began to offer our employees bonuses. I think they would have worked just as hard without the bonuses because of who they were, but just as they wanted more than mere survival, we needed them for the long haul.

As a result of our collective actions, although it took us three years to be fully set up in a new building, we did not miss a step in growing our business.

To put our achievement in perspective, in 1972, we had six employees, and in 1979, the year of the fire, the number of employees was over 25. Between 1979 and 1982, when we moved into our new facility, we more than doubled both the revenue for our company and our employee base.

Focus, on the other hand, was much harder to achieve. I knew we would not be distracted from meeting our customers' needs, but exactly which needs would we meet and how? No business can do everything, and those that try do so at their own peril. We had created the mobility market, and it was up to us to decide on how much of it we'd pursue.

By this time, our lift operations, both consumer and commercial, accounted for the majority of our business. The Tri-Wheeler portion of our business was slightly but steadily shrinking, at no more than 10 percent of our overall revenue. Would we continue to offer both lifts and Tri-Wheelers? The lift business had a higher margin and promised good growth because medical advances meant people were living longer and overcoming disabilities that would have sidelined them in years past. We were already the market leader in lifts and van conversions, and we were making a much better product than our competitors. We also were in the midst of developing a strong dealer network that would greatly increase the reach of our products. There was no reason to stop selling lifts.

Tri-Wheelers presented a different case. Though our motorized wheelchair was far superior to others on the market and we had been the first company to offer the product, we faced some tough challenges. For one thing, dozens of companies were offering scooters at that point. For another, the manufacturing of these wheelchairs had gone overseas to utilize cheap labor.

These two factors combined drove the price down dramatically, and when that happened, the quality went with it. Our motorized Tri-Wheelers were manufactured in Winamac and were still predominately custom-made. This meant our chairs, while much better than our competitors', cost more. Moreover, because of our labor and material costs, our profit margin was miniscule. When you considered the fact that more of our resources would need to go to the manufacturing of lifts and conversions of vans, it all added up to an easy decision, right?

Not so fast. Many of our lift customers started out with Tri-Wheelers, and when we expanded our product line to include lifts, they came with us. Our Tri-Wheelers had been an important part of bridging from our past to our future. Because I invented the Tri-Wheeler, there was an emotional connection as well. By giving myself the gift of mobility, I was able to help other people live more active and able lives, and to me, that had its own currency. Having said all of that, business was business, and as a CEO, I had to make a call.

I decided we would, over a few years, transition out of making Tri-Wheelers. We would continue to service our existing Tri-Wheeler customers but focus our research and development on lifts and van conversions. I also decided to make a supply of the scooters for myself so I would never have to go without. To this day, I still tinker with the design of my Tri-Wheelers and make improvements on them from time to time, but I can honestly say I made the right decision to exit that part of the business.

Another decision, which was really a continuation of an existing practice, was to make a major upgrade to our production capabilities. We knew the only way we could stay in business—especially with lifts and vans, which were much more sophisticated than Tri-Wheelers—was to stay on top of the latest technology and work with it. Otherwise, we'd get left behind.

After surviving the fire and overcoming numerous other challenges, I was going to do everything in my power to keep us from falling behind. The drive I had was for more than me alone; it was also for my employees. We were like pieces of pottery in one simple way: we had gone through a fire together, and while we may have had some cracks in us as a result, in my mind, we were all stronger for the experience.

chapter sixteen

OUT OF THE ASHES

*Don't go around saying the world owes
you a living; the world owes you nothing;
it was here first.*

-- Mark Twain

A FEW of my colleagues and I were reminiscing the other day about how we overcame the fire that nearly destroyed our company.

Someone brought up the ancient legend of the Phoenix, a mythological bird that lived for 500 years, died in a fire, and then came back stronger, only to do it all over again 500 years later. I don't like that story. First, I never want to go through a fire again. Second, people forget the Phoenix built its own funeral pyre, and that's something I have no interest in—ever.

Another person talked about the Thunderbird, which is the Native American version of the Phoenix. In that legend, a powerful spirit takes the form of a bird that waters the earth, beats its wings to cause rolling thunder, and shoots lightning from its beak. I like the idea of a strong creature that helps people, and I loved the Thunderbird car, but I associate lightning with fire. Not for me.

Finally, another colleague offered a thought more in keeping with the spirit of our company: we were not content to sit on our ashes. It was not in our makeup and never would be.

After the fire, we started to get more complex and creative in our designs and engineering, and, consequently, we needed equipment that could help us produce what we had in mind. Let me try to provide a snapshot of some of the technology investments we made during this rebuilding period.

We bought state-of-the-art MIG (metal inert gas) welders to replace our older welders. They were big and more advanced in technology and were twice as expensive as the earlier models, but they greatly improved our productivity and cut costs.

We bought a brake press, which cut metal, and a brake shear, which bent the metal, for a total of $50,000.

We bought our first metal lathe, from John Mahan, which was a well-used piece of equipment that he had discarded from his manufacturing facility. Later, we purchased three Wasino metal lathes.

We bought our first turret punch press, from Warner & Swayze, for about $125,000. It increased our speed and flexibility, eliminated hard tooling, and enabled us to program the setup through a computer. This was revolutionary technology, and the machine was as big as a car, but we had to have it. Later, we bought two more turret punch presses, trade show demos from Wiedemann that cost about $175,000 each. They were even bigger than the prior ones from Warner & Swayze, about the size of pickup trucks.

Then, we bought two Mazak lasers at another $250,000 apiece. They had all the same labor and productivity improvements but also enabled us to cut shapes quickly. By the mid-'90s, we had added seven Trumpf lasers, each bought at a cost of about $500,000.

Painting was another area of technology investment for us. In the early days, back in my parents' garage, I had started out with a cup gun, which is what auto body repair shops use. I would build the lifts on a fixture that took the place of an actual van, take them to Fritz's Body Shop for painting, bring the lifts home and disassemble them, wrap the pieces in newspaper, and then ship them off. The buyer on the other end would do the assembly. Over the years, we went back and forth between shipping the lifts assembled and disassembled, and each time it affected how we painted the lifts and even how we built them. In the end, we improved with each change.

In the mid-1970s, we graduated to a $600 airless spray gun system from Graco, which I learned about after watching people from Allis Chalmers paint grain elevators in a leaky, drafty, and freezing-cold building that had been part of the old Studebaker buildings in South Bend, Indiana, before the auto manufacturer closed. I figured if they could make that paint system work in an environment like that, surely it would work for me. For paint, we used a "battleship gray" color of paint purchased from Elpaco Coatings Corporation in Elkhart, Indiana. After the fire, we added "platinum" and "toast" colors.

The airless spray gun system worked well for us until a few years after the fire, when we invested $500,000 in a new powder-coating system. Powder coating was relatively new and expensive, and as a result, not many people were using it. However, because the process offered a more durable finish, production flexibility, and environmental friendliness, we wanted to determine whether it might be suitable for us.

To see it in action, we flew to Moundridge, Kansas, where Grasshopper Lawn Mowers had installed the system in 1986.

When we arrived, we were picked up in an old pickup truck with flame decals, a gun rack in the window, an engine that roared, and dual exhaust pipes that constantly belched thick black smoke. It definitely provided an interesting contrast to the expensive system we were about to see—while at the same time illustrating how poorly prepared society was in providing accessibility for the disabled. I couldn't get my Tri-Wheeler on the plane, so I had to use a manual wheelchair, and the three people accompanying me had to hoist me up into the bed of the truck by hand. Without a way to tie my chair down, Jeff Hermanson stuck his foot in between the spokes to keep me from rolling away. It's a wonder he didn't lose his foot, or at least some toes, in the process—or, worse yet, *me* out the back end of the pickup truck.

If the trip out to the factory was dicey, what we saw inside was anything but. The company had transitioned from wet paint to powder coating just one year earlier, so the experience was fresh and very useful to us. What's more, throughout the year, they switched back and forth between painting lawn mowers and garden cultivators, so we could see how flexible and sophisticated the process was. Satisfied with what we had seen, we swallowed hard, placed our order with the salesman, and went back to Winamac. We still use the system today and continually improve it as our needs evolve.

Regarding information technology, prior to the fire, our general manager was a manual accounting person and did everything by hand. I was intrigued by the promise of computing and was eager to see what it could do, so I started using a TRS-80 microcomputer from Radio Shack and then an Apple II, both in the family room at my house, before graduating in 1981 to a Qantel QMRP.

People laugh when I tell them about my TRS-80, but that computer, the most expensive product Radio Shack had ever sold up to that point, was quite a success. Designed to compete against

Apple and Commodore, the TRS-80 sold for $599 and included the computer, monitor, keyboard, and cassette storage. As the story goes, after the press conference announcing the computer's introduction, critics formed a sharp difference of opinion regarding the machine's prospects. The inventors of the TRS-80 said at least 50,000 would be sold; management said the number would be closer to 1,000. Management was quickly proven wrong: in the next five months, they sold 65,000 and by 1981, 250,000. As someone who is comfortable being on the cutting edge of new technology, I loved that computer. Looking back, I especially love the fact that the inventors were proven right and the computer far exceeded management's estimates. Score one for the underdogs.

After the TRS-80, I moved to the Apple II. Also introduced in 1977, the Apple II was even more successful than the TRS-80, selling approximately 7 million units by 1993, the year it ceased production. Because it was designed for home use, the Apple II was often the first computer anyone had ever seen up close. At $1,298, it was more expensive than its competitors but still affordable for many middle-class families. With built-in BASIC programming, a color monitor, expansion slots, a case, and a keyboard, the Apple II was more user-friendly than the other computers on the market. What made Apple II sales go through the roof was its new spreadsheet program, VisiCalc, which added columns and rows of data, much like Microsoft's Excel does today. It became a serious business machine as well as a home computer.

Perhaps the best part about my Apple II was that I got it for free. By selling so many Dodge vans, Chrysler gave me coupons and a catalog and said I could take my pick of golf clubs, a boat, a barbeque grill, and other items. Because I didn't have much use for those things, I got the computer and put it through its paces trying to extract information that would make my company perform more efficiently.

In 1981, after about three years, we outgrew the Apple II and bought a Qantel QMRP, which was a powerful, fully integrated software system popular with manufacturers at the time. While the $40,000 purchase price was a big investment, we got our money's worth before we switched to a client/server configuration in 1999.

Qantel was a relatively young and scrappy company—much like we were—started by a group of former engineers from Singer's computer division in Hayward, California. IBM was the 800-pound gorilla in the market, but when Qantel's first product was launched in 1969, *Computerworld* hailed it as "a computer practically small enough to slip into a suitcase, powerful enough to handle many business applications, and less expensive than a sports car." The company's upstart status, and the fact that its reliable, continually updated technology was geared more toward manufacturers, made it a good fit for our company, until we outgrew it as well.

I think it's important to note that all of these infrastructure investments, from production machinery and painting systems to information technology, were cutting-edge at the time, but they were also complementary. This meant we continued to utilize everything we invested in to meet our demand—in fact, we still do. Nothing is ever really obsolete; we simply use and improve what we have so we can constantly increase our capability and our capacity. As a result, our equipment has long since paid for itself in cost savings and quality.

This brings up another issue, one that all CEOs confront as they plan their operations and one I faced when I considered how to rebuild after the fire. Simply put, in order to have the capabilities needed to properly run your business, how do you decide whether you should build capability yourself, purchase it through investments and acquisitions, or partner with another company that perhaps has part of what you need? The best way I can answer that is to say it's a strategic question without one right answer. The decision is dependent on a combination of factors, and it changes as each situation evolves. Having said that, I will add this: our overriding philosophy has always been that if we need or want something, we first look to see whether we can make it ourselves.

A case in point is our hydraulic cylinders, which we manufacture at our plant in Winamac. We build them ourselves for a number of reasons. First and foremost, we know that because of their unique circumstances, our disabled customers need to feel—beyond a shadow of a doubt—they can trust our products to be reliable, long lasting, and completely safe. Every company should strive for those attributes in their products, but with us it's especially so. If a lift or a ramp on one of our vehicles doesn't work, wears out, or is unstable, our customers may have a harder time finding help. If our products are unreliable, our customers are stuck or, worse, in danger. Because I am in a chair and rely on lifts and ramps myself, I happen to have firsthand knowledge of why this is so important. That's why our cylinders, as part of the "special sauce" of our company, are important enough for us to build ourselves.

Second, building our own cylinders makes economic sense. Because we're out in the middle of a cornfield, we don't have job shops nearby that we can easily call on to do manufacturing for us. Because we don't buy parts in large enough quantities to achieve economies of scale from some distant manufacturer, purchasing our cylinders elsewhere is cost prohibitive. By buying the raw materials and making the parts ourselves, we can reduce our manufacturing and procurement costs and pass the value on to our customers.

Finally, making our own cylinders gives us a competitive advantage. We've seen too many companies get in trouble because they use parts that are cheaply made. They may be good enough for snowplows or farm machinery, but they do not provide the quality we demand for our products to help customers feel safe and secure. In contrast, we strive to produce the same kind of ultraprecision equipment used in airplanes, which have no room for error. We are unique in this regard because not only were we the first lift manufacturer to make our own hydraulic cylinders, starting in 1983, but also, to this day, we're the only one.

Did we invest in all of this sophisticated production equipment, painting systems, and information technology and then discover that these things enabled us to manufacture ultraprecision products? Or were we already making great products but needed to have an infrastructure that could keep pace with our vision? Of course, the answers are yes to both. Our infrastructure was and is a constantly evolving environment that balances capability with demand. Out of that environment grows new infrastructure needs and also new advances in engineering and design. They feed each other, which was exactly the case when we switched from a one-at-a-time manufacturing process to an assembly line in the mid-1980s.

As we rebuilt and demand continued to soar, we constantly had to figure out how to satisfy that demand within the space that we occupied. Because the business next door to us was only six feet away from our back door, we were running out of floor space. As a result, we had to look for ways to reduce the space it took to do things while still keeping up with the volume that was needed.

We hired some consultants to help us think through our situation, but at the end of the process, they had to admit that our experience had given us a unique insight into how we should do things. By not trying to force some costly and complicated system on us, they gave us some priceless advice: we should always remember that we know more about our customers' mobility needs than anyone else, and because of that knowledge, we should have faith that our instincts would lead us to make the right choices.

Were those consultants shirking their duties because they could not provide us with an adequate solution? Quite the opposite—they were acknowledging something we needed to believe ourselves: we had become a grown-up company poised for a future even more remarkable than its past, and that was saying something.

I'd like to make one final note about resiliency, and it's of a personal nature. Sometimes in life, even though we work hard to make a success of something, we come up short. Such was the case with my marriage to my high school sweetheart.

After many years of struggling, I made the hardest decision of my life, to end my marriage to Linda. Some years later, she passed away from a massive heart attack and left me as the sole parent of our five children.

After my divorce, I was very apprehensive about becoming involved in another relationship, but then I met Melody. She lived in a nearby town and had been widowed for several years.

The story of how we got together is interesting. Melody was an interior decorator and was trying to find a model airplane propeller for a project she was hired to complete. A relative of hers suggested she call me to see whether I could help her out, because I've always been a model plane enthusiast.

As we got to know each other, we discovered we had a lot in common. She came with me to a Colts football game, and not only did the Colts win that day but so did I. A few years later, we were married.

Like the Indianapolis Colts, who later won the Super Bowl in 2006, I was making a comeback both at work and at home.

RISE ABOVE

My employees and I celebrate the latest redesign of the
Tri-Wheeler in the late 1970s.

Beginning production in the early 1980s, paratransit vans finally allowed people
with disabilities access to public transportation.

RISE ABOVE

*How one man's search for mobility
helped the world get moving*

After Congress passed the Education for All Handicapped Children Act
in 1975, Braun competed to secure a dominant share of the school bus
market with the new Lift-A-Way lift.

This marketing photo from the late 1980s features the
Lift-A-Way and the Swing-A-Way wheelchair lifts.

As the company grew, I continued to invest in the latest manufacturing technology to keep up with demand and ensure the highest quality products.

In the late 1970s, I expanded my manufacturing capabilities to include a variety of fiberglass products, from wheelchair van tops to portable toilets to the wheelchair-accessible Roll-In shower.

Braun's new Roll-in...
because taking a shower should be easy

RISE ABOVE

How one man's search for mobility
helped the world get moving

Braun Corporation's international market continues to grow

The company slowly began to expand into international markets in the 1980s. Today, Braun products are available around the world.

Chrysler Honors Braun Van

2-15-84

A redesigned, custom van by Braun Corporation took top honors in a recent Chrysler Corporation contest in the disabled person conversion category.

The van, called the "Braun Wheelchair Caravan," was selected by Chrysler's product development department in the international competition.

President of Braun Corporation, Ralph Braun, said engineers designed the conversion van with the handicapped consumer and paratransit adaptations in mind.

Braun said engineers separated the van at midpoint, lengthening the vehicle by 18 inches. He said increasing the length of the van would allow for a larger doorway.

Because of the interior height of the van, Braun raised the roof and entrance door for better accesibility. Even with the higher roof, the van can fit inside a standard seven-foot garage.

A five-inch power elevator was added to the driver compartment to allow the driver to operate the vehicle while seated in his wheel chair. Driver hand controls and several other options were added in the final stage of production.

A standard rear, or third seat was modified to fold upright and wheelchair tie-downs were fastened to the chair. The seat can be used by two

A completed Braun van conversion

adult passengers or as a wheelchair tie-down position. A second wheelchair tie-down position was located behind the driver facing the lift.

The Braun Corporation is recognized as the world leader in the production and sales of wheelchair lifts for the handicapped. Braun headquaters are in Winamac, with additional plants and sales offices in Huntington Beach, Calif., and Clearwater, Fla.

Chrysler introduced the first minivan in 1984, and my team and I immediately set to work making it accessible. The revolutionary lowered-floor Entervan conversion was still a few years away.

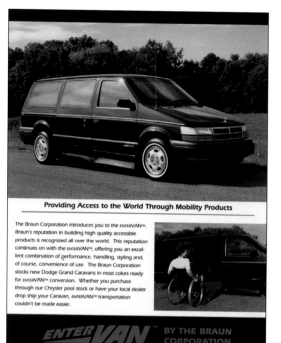

Introduced in the late 1980s, the Entervan soon became the flagship of the Braun fleet. The lowered floor and ramp offered unprecedented ease of access for wheelchair users.

Providing Access to the World Through Mobility Products

The Braun Corporation introduces you to the ENTERVAN™. Braun's reputation in building high quality accessible products is recognized all over the world. This reputation continues on with the ENTERVAN™, offering you an excellent combination of performance, handling, styling and, of course, convenience of use. The Braun Corporation stocks new Dodge Grand Caravans in most colors ready for ENTERVAN™ conversion. Whether you purchase through our Chrysler pool stock or have your local dealer drop ship your Caravan, ENTERVAN™ transportation couldn't be made easier.

ENTER*VAN*™ BY THE BRAUN CORPORATION

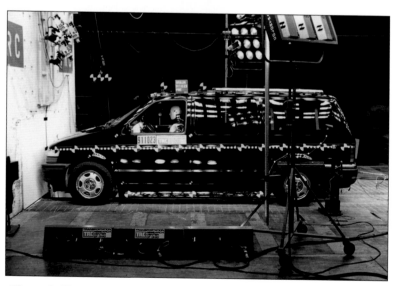

The early Entervan conversion was impact-tested to comply with Federal Motor Vehicle Safety Standards. This focus on safety continues today with each redesign of the Entervan and Rampvan.

RISE ABOVE

How one man's search for mobility helped the world get moving

The company added a 210,000 sq. ft. production facility in the early 1990s to accommodate vehicle production and the new corporate headquarters.

Me posing for a marketing photo with a 2000 model year Dodge Entervan. At this time minivans had been in production for over a decade, and the Braun engineers continued their ongoing efforts to refine and improve the design.

Me and the Toyota Sienna production crew with customer Barbara Reed's Rampvan as it rolls off the assembly line.

An aerial view of vehicle production facilities— then and now—showing vans awaiting conversion. Completed wheelchair vans are shipped to BraunAbility dealerships across the country.

RISE ABOVE

*How one man's search for mobility
helped the world get moving*

Despite the global reach of BraunAbility, I still interact with my customers regularly at every opportunity. Here I am with the "Ultimate Fan Van Giveaway" winner, Kody Harlow and family.

The company that I started in my parents' garage has kept its roots in the town of Winamac, Indiana, (pop. 2,500). Today BraunAbility has over 700 employees.

chapter seventeen

BACK TO SCHOOL

*In business, the competition will bite you
if you keep on running, if you stand still,
they will swallow you.*

-- Victor Kiam

AS MY father said, in the ladder of life, you're either climbing up or you're sliding down. Which way you go is up to you. I learned from him the importance of surrounding yourself with good people who will help you in your climb and of helping others in theirs.

When it comes to business competitors, here's what I think about that ladder: no matter which rung you're on, if you're climbing up, your competitors are going to stomp on your fingers, pull on your legs, and try to shake you to the ground.

Wait a minute, you say. Isn't this a heartwarming story of inspiration, of rising above challenges, of giving people the ability to live the lives they want to live?

Well, I hope it is. But it is also a story with one undeniable reality: business can be a knock-down, drag-out, bare-knuckled brawl where one side wins and the other side loses. It doesn't have to be, and in theory, you should be able to peacefully compete against, buy from, sell to, and partner with any company with which you have a common interest. Unfortunately, while that's a nice theory, at some point, competition means somebody wins and somebody loses. If you're in business, you know what I mean. If you're not, consider what Ray Kroc, founder of McDonald's, had to say on the subject: "If any of my competitors were drowning, I'd stick a hose in their mouth and turn on the water."

Pretty far from warm and fuzzy.

Don't get me wrong: competitors serve a useful purpose. They make you think about where you're strong and where you're weak. They make you focus on your goals and then give you the incentive to keep going until you've reached those goals. They make you hire good people and then constantly figure out how to keep those people. They make you think creatively and then manifest that creativity with action and execution. They make you pay attention to your customers' needs and then work to ensure their satisfaction. With every aspect of your business, competitors make you stronger.

I accept competition as a fact of life, and I even respect what it can do for my business, but I don't have to like it.

In my youth, my first competitor was muscular dystrophy, followed closely thereafter by the diminished expectations of society. Because I had been diagnosed with muscular dystrophy, people said I'd never amount to anything. Letting my diagnosis defeat me would have been easy, but I couldn't accept that.

In my battle against muscular dystrophy, I won as best I could.

When I started my business, I competed against the banker who wouldn't give me a loan, the local businessmen who thought "those boys in the wheelchairs" would never make it, and the suppliers who somehow thought my being in a chair meant they could take advantage of me.

In my battle against society's small-minded, I won.

As my business grew out of infancy, I competed against those who wanted to lure away my customers—whether they bought my Tri-Wheelers or converted vans and lifts—and who used cheap, poorly built products to cut into my market share.

In my battle against business competitors, I've won far more often than I've lost.

From Frankenstein and my postal Jeep to the hundreds of thousands of products that have gone out our doors, I've always had a special interest in protecting, nurturing, and growing the mobility industry. It's not merely that I didn't want anyone to take it away from me; I just didn't want anyone to do it halfheartedly or for the wrong purpose. Customers who need mobility products can't afford to put their trust in shoddy products offered by people who want to make a quick buck. As a CEO, and also as someone who lives life in a chair, I guess you could say I've always felt protective of the disabled community. Perhaps that's partly why my battles against business competitors have been so intense.

A case in point is the school bus segment of our business. I will recount a competitive experience I had in this arena, but first, let me offer some perspective as to why this battle was so important.

School busing is a critical and large part of educational eco-systems all over the world, and it is especially so in the United States. Just as our nation's schools must adhere to strict regulations mandated by the Americans with Disabilities Act (ADA) of 1990 and other rules regarding students with special needs and disabilities, so, too, must school buses.

As a market segment, school busing is big and getting bigger. With the population in the United States growing dramatically, school buses now give children more than 10 billion rides to and from school each year.

Let me provide some historical perspective. About 140 years ago, Massachusetts became the first state to enact legislation permitting public funds to be spent on transporting children to school. In converted wagons used on farms, these canvass-covered "school wagons" carried nineteenth-century children to and from the surrounding countryside to more centrally located schools.

Fifty years later, the rest of the states passed similar laws. When they did, the concept of the modern school bus was born as steel-bodied motorized trucks began to take the place of the outmoded horse-drawn school wagons. What was the reason for this evolution? Education was becoming a national strategic imperative, a notion supported by the states' efforts to consolidate schools and mandate attendance during this period.

By 1950, when I was 10 years old, approximately 115,000 American school buses carried 7 million students—excluding me and other disabled kids—to school. In 1975, those numbers skyrocketed when Congress passed the Education for All Handicapped Children Act, which required all federally funded public schools to provide transportation to and from school for children with physical and mental disabilities. Today, at a cost of about $500 per year per student, approximately 23 million children, many with special needs, travel nearly 4 billion miles on about 450,000 school buses.

There is a great irony in this. As a young student, I was unable to benefit from this kind of accessible transportation, but as an adult, I get a lot of satisfaction out of knowing that a good majority of those school buses use my company's lifts. In short, while school taught me nothing about competition, competition taught me plenty about school. I put that education to good use.

In the mid-1970s, we created our first lift for vehicles with high floors. When the Education for All Handicapped Children Act passed, we knew school buses had the potential to give us a good amount of growth, and we thought our new lift would position us nicely for that market.

At the time, we were selling quite a lot of our new lifts through Mobile Tech, a division of Collins Industries that had already been making small school buses for a couple of years and had some knowledge of the industry. All was going well, and both of our companies were making progress—until one day when the president of Collins Industries, Don Collins, came to Winamac to take Burnie Blackmon and me out to dinner. At dinner, I got a real taste of what competition was all about.

As our dinner was winding down and Don pushed away his plate, he lit a big, fat cigar and sat back in his chair.

He patted and rubbed his belly. "Ralph, we've been doing pretty good together, haven't we?" he asked.

"Yes, we've been doing all right," I answered.

"Well, I think we can do better," he said. "I think there's a lot of room for growth. You agree?"

"Sure," I said. "I think the market has a lot of potential."

"I've been thinking," he continued, "and I think there's only one way we're going to grab this thing and really make it work."

"What do you have in mind?" I asked.

He puffed on his cigar a couple of times and blew a thick plume of blue smoke toward the ceiling. Then, he leaned toward me and grinned with what seemed like hundreds of sharp teeth.

"Ralph, I have a proposition for you," he said. "I want to buy your little company here, fold it into Mobile Tech, and move it to Kansas, with the rest of my businesses. What do you think about that?"

I was stunned. He acted like he'd just given me a birthday present, like I should be shouting with joy, relieved of a burden and grateful for his generosity. Just a minute earlier, we were business partners, doing well together.

I looked at Burnie and turned back to Don. "We're not for sale."

With that, his entire demeanor changed.

He scowled and pointed the tip of his cigar at me. "Listen, you're charging me way too much for those lifts, and neither of us is making what we should," he said, now with a different tone in his voice. "Now, you know I don't need you, because I can make these things myself. But I thought I'd do you a favor. I thought I'd take this thing off your hands and get it out of this damn cornfield and over to Hutchinson where it belongs."

"You don't need me, but you just offered to buy my company," I said. "There's something wrong with that picture, don't you think?"

"I didn't offer to buy your company," he sneered. "I *told* you I'd buy your company."

"And I *told you* we're not for sale," I said.

Don was accustomed to getting his way, and with my flat-out "no," his face changed from white to red to purple in seconds.

I continued, "I'll tell you what I'll do. You say you're paying too much for my lifts. Well, what do you think a fair price is?"

Now he was seething. "You don't get it. I can build a better lift myself and beat the pants off you!"

"Then go ahead and build it," I said, turning to Burnie. "We're done here." I began to back up my chair.

"Now hold on a minute," he said. "What do you mean 'We're done'?"

"That's it," I said, with finality. "C'mon, Burnie."

He snorted a sarcastic laugh and sat back in his chair. Grinning again, he said, "Well, boys, if that's how it's gonna be, I'm afraid I'm gonna have to put you out of business."

As Burnie and I went toward the door, Don, aware that his final attempt at bullying had failed, yelled at our backs, "Ralph? Ralph! HEY!"

We kept right on going. Outside, I had that old familiar feeling: I'll show him.

A few months after that episode, we took one of our new lifts to see a purchasing agent at the Wayne Corporation, a large bus manufacturer in Richmond, Indiana. Collins Industries hadn't been our only customer for our school bus lifts, but without that company on board, we needed to expand our reach. Wayne had been in the school bus business since the 1800s, back when school buses were the horse-drawn wagons I described earlier, so it had deep knowledge of the industry and seemed like a good fit. What's more, Don Collins had started selling his own lifts directly to Wayne, and we had heard his lifts had issues with quality and reliability. Plain and simple, they were cheaply made, and school districts were complaining about them.

Because we did not have a school bus on which we could demonstrate the lift, we installed it on the back of a pickup truck. The purchasing agent, a short, roly-poly man with red hair, watched as our lift worked perfectly. His nickname was Red, because not only was his hair red but I believe he also chewed Red Man tobacco.

Red liked what he saw. When we finished our sales pitch, he asked how much we wanted for it. When I told him, the atmosphere changed, much like it had with Don Collins.

Red paused, walked to where I was sitting, leaned over me in my chair, and said, his voice dripping with condescension, "You don't actually think I'm going to pay that much for that thing, now do you?" As he spoke, some spit flew out of his mouth and landed on my face. It was unintentional, but the combination of his condescending attitude, his tobacco-laced spittle, and the fact we were sitting in a parking lot on a sweltering hot day didn't sit well with me. I was there to make a sale, so I forged ahead. I told him, with all the politeness I could muster, that I thought we had priced it fairly because it was much higher quality than the Collins product they were using, and I knew how much material and labor costs went into manufacturing. Undeterred, he bid us goodbye, and we went back to Winamac.

Three years later, we finally made the sale. In the interim, we learned that Collins had shut us out of the market by cutting deals with all of the bus manufacturers to make sure their lifts were the ones being installed in their buses. They were willing to go with the cheaply built, poor-quality product because they could make such a high margin selling them. We were stuck and needed to find another way into the market.

We decided to change our go-to-market strategy and directly approach the dealers who served the school districts. It worked, for one main reason: the complaints about our competitor's quality were getting louder and more frequent, and their business was hurting. Because the school bus dealers were the ones who dealt with the school districts on a day-to-day basis, they got the brunt of the criticism, despite the fact they weren't the manufacturers of the buses or the lifts that were in them.

One of those dealers was Bob Matthews, who was buying his buses from Thomas Built, a large manufacturer out of High Point, North Carolina, that was using Collins's lifts. Bob came to see us in Winamac because the quality issue was getting out of hand.

The school districts depended on him to deliver quality products that lasted, and he wanted to make things right. Rather than make me travel to New York, he flew to Winamac in his private plane, where I picked him up and brought him to the plant.

Within an hour of watching our lifts in action and hearing us talk about the care and effort we put into making them, Bob was sold. He wasted no time in placing an order for 55 lifts. Next, instead of waiting for the lifts to be shipped, he said he would bring 55 buses all the way to Winamac so we could install the lifts ourselves. Now this was a man of action—my kind of guy.

Bob was getting his buses from Thomas Built, who had been buying and installing Collins's lifts, putting in doors, and then shipping the completed buses to his dealership in New York. Because Thomas Built had made a deal with Collins and wouldn't buy our lifts, Bob bypassed them by going to us directly. As a result, 55 buses came to Winamac with Thomas Built's doors, but they went back to Bob with 55 Braun lifts.

After the first 55 buses, we started shipping our lifts as kits to Bob, who then began installing them at his own facility. It took a while for Thomas Built to figure out that although the same amount of buses was being shipped, a number of them didn't have any lifts in them. As word got around that Bob was taking the direct route to get our lifts, other school bus dealers began to follow suit. Soon, more bus manufacturers were watching their buses go out the door, minus any lifts, along with revenue they would have previously gotten. The Wayne Corporation was one of them. That's when I got a call from Red, the purchasing agent from Wayne, who this time had a decidedly different tone. He was missing a lot of revenue and wanted to make a deal.

The bus manufacturers had taken five years to decide they'd better jump on the bandwagon and start using our lifts. Ultimately, our lifts began going to all of the bus manufacturers, and they still do today. We had to go through the back door to get there, but it was worth it.

Fast-forward all the way to 1997. Don Collins had tried in vain to beat me with Mobile Tech in the school bus lift business. He had also tried and failed to get into my consumer business of converting vans. Finally, he retired and left the business to his son, also named Don. In an effort to hang on and get back at me, Junior had seen a Swedish design from UVL, makers of under-vehicle lifts—lifts stored under vehicles instead of inside them—and decided to copy the design and manufacture the lifts through Mobile Tech.

UVL had a nice design and very good lifts, but when Junior tried to reengineer the lifts so he could avoid paying royalties on the patent, he ended up making an inferior product and still infringed on the patent. I had heard about this and knew UVL's design was strong, so I bought the UVL patent for our company. When I did, I informed Junior and Mobile Tech they were infringing on our newly acquired patent and would have to pay us royalties. He was not at all happy. However, he knew he could not afford to make the royalty payments and also realized Mobile Tech did not fit within Collins Industries' long-term strategy. He was in a jam with no way out.

I called Junior and offered him a deal: instead of going into a long and costly legal battle over the patent infringement, I would buy Mobile Tech and enable Collins Industries to focus on its core business. Defeated, Junior gritted his teeth and made the deal.

After I hung up the phone, I smiled with satisfaction. Alone in my office, I realized how far I'd come from the restaurant that night when Don Collins Sr. told me either I was going to sell him my company or he was going to put me out of business. Having fought the battle and won, I felt victorious.

I turned to leave my office and move on to the next challenge, but before I did, I took one last look at the phone and said to the empty room: "Twenty-five years ago you poked your cigar at me and said you were going to put me out of business. You failed, and I'm still here. Welcome to the big leagues. Welcome to the cornfield."

chapter eighteen

IT'S A SMALL WORLD

A good product knows no national boundaries.
-- Hideo Sugiura, Former Honda Chairman

EARLY IN the life of our business, when the first lift customers were coming to Indiana from Texas, Massachusetts, and other areas of the country, I knew our products would have wide appeal everywhere we offered them—and not just in the United States. After all, disability doesn't care where you live, and neither should mobility.

As a smaller, more nimble entrepreneurial company, extending our reach across international borders made sense. By going into other geographies, we could tap into local markets that otherwise would not have been available to us. I'd read that 75 percent of U.S. exports came from small businesses; if that were true, why couldn't ours be one of them?

I asked myself, Where should we go, how would we get there, and when?

While we didn't begin our overseas expansion until the 1980s and our products are now available most everywhere in the world, the seeds were planted a full 10 years earlier when I got a call from a paraplegic former U.S. Air Force fighter pilot living in Canada. He had seen my ad in *Accent on Living* and thought I might be able to convert his new Dodge van on his drive south from Canada to Costa Rica to spend the winter.

Like the story of Don Collins, this one is a cautionary tale that took many years and numerous twists and was a contributing factor behind our move to open a facility in Florida, after which California, New Jersey, and overseas countries quickly followed.

The disabled veteran pilot had a camper conversion in his Dodge van and planned to sleep in it on his way south to Costa Rica. He wanted to sleep in it in my parents' garage while we installed a lift for him. When I asked him how he was going to pay for it, he said the VA would send me a check for the full amount. This was the first-ever sale to the VA on behalf of a Vietnam veteran, so I did not know what to make of it in the beginning.

While he slept in his van in the garage for the two weeks I worked, I talked to the VA and exchanged a lot of paperwork. Finally, I was convinced there was a good possibility I would get paid for it. I reasoned that if the VA funded the conversion, with the amount of veterans who were returning home disabled, this would set a precedent and open the door to even more of these deals as time went on.

I finished the job and sent the pilot on his way to Costa Rica. Before he left, he gave me a personal check and told me not to cash it unless the money did not come in from the VA. He said he knew a lot of people in Washington, and I knew he had a tremendous gift of manipulation, so I thought if anybody could get the funding, it would be him.

Two months later, I got the check from the VA and a call from the pilot. He had been thinking the same way I had; if the VA had paid for his van conversion, with the amount of disabled veterans out there, a lot more funding would be available. He had an idea: he would buy a bunch of vans and ship them to me in Winamac for conversion, and then he would sell them under the name Speedy Wagon. It sounded like a viable plan to me and another route to market for my lifts, albeit under a private label, so I agreed to it.

Within two months, he started running advertisements in *Accent on Living*—to compete against me. They ran on facing pages, and both ads featured the same product, with one difference: he doubled his photograph so it looked like he had twice as many vans as me. Our customers were, understandably, very confused.

This odd competition went on for a year or so, but I kept converting his vans because it was also helping me grow my business. Then the relationship started to get a little squishy. His customers started calling me directly because he had promised them earlier delivery, custom work, and other things that we hadn't agreed upon. He also started stringing me along on his payments; he was floating my money.

I started to back away from the relationship. When I did, the pilot started buying electric lifts from a man in Canada by smuggling them across the border late at night, driving them to a plant in St. Louis, and installing them. Before long, he had really cut into my business from the VA.

Not long after, the pilot started to string along the Canadian lift manufacturer, and their relationship turned sour. When the Canadian man ended that relationship, the pilot took the electric lift to a machine shop and had it reverse-engineered; in other words, he copied it. But when he copied it, he cut corners and used cheaper materials, and as a result, it got butchered.

As if that weren't enough, the pilot stuck it to the people in St. Louis, left them in the middle of the night, and set up shop near Tampa, Florida. There, he again had some knockoff lifts made. This resulted in yet another drop in quality, untold amounts of dissatisfied customers, and a very unhappy VA, which had funded all of those van conversions and was constantly getting calls from veterans stranded by malfunctioning lifts. It was a disaster, and the VA asked for our help.

We set up shop in the Tampa area and went to work. Immediately upon our arrival, there was a parade of Speedy Wagons coming to us. All day, for weeks on end, we cut out their lifts and replaced them with ours. Within a very short period of time, we took all of the pilot's customers and put him out of business. He still was not done causing damage, because before he went out of business, he stopped honoring the warranties on his vehicles. This was fraud, and when the VA sent out a warrant for his arrest, he fled again under cover of night to Canada, where he stayed. He had left a nine-year path of destruction in his wake, but at least he was gone.

Gone, that is, until I saw him again at a campground in Florida in 2003. We had a cordial conversation, and in an odd twist of fate, he told me we'd actually been servicing his Braun lift for many years, often on his way to and from Costa Rica. Because I had no reason to open up old wounds and talk about all he had done—and, obviously, neither did he—we parted ways amicably. We weren't friends, but we weren't enemies, either. As I left the campground that day, I was struck by the thought that even one of my most energetic former competitors could become a customer, proving once again that disability and mobility know no boundaries, geographic or otherwise.

Of course, the pilot was not the only reason we went to Florida. The state has always been a popular destination for retirees in general. Since the end of World War II, veterans have been drawn to Florida because of its warm weather, relatively low taxes, extensive services, and large military community. Twenty years from now, due to a huge influx of soldiers returning from Afghanistan and Iraq, experts predict that Florida will overtake California as the state with the largest population of military veterans. In the 1980s, because our competitors were beginning to cut into our business in California, that state became the next stop on our expansion agenda.

As is often the case, our expansion plans coincided with someone on the outside who wanted to get involved with our business. In this case, a man with polio was eking out a living by installing hand controls in cars out of a small garage in California, and he approached us about installing our lifts. After we struck a deal, he came to Indiana to learn how to put them into vans.

We began shipping him lifts he could install in California, and before long, his business started to take off. However, there was one very big problem: he was a wild hare, and he had no interest in running a business. Instead, he wanted to party. I found this out the hard way, when I made a trip to California to see him and his operation. He would come in to work late in the morning, have a two-martini lunch at noon, and then adjourn to his house at 3:00 for some serious drinking. At 7:00, he would have dinner and two more martinis. After dinner, it kept going. Then the next day, he would get up and do the same thing all over again. I was never much of a drinker, but I could tell right away this was going to be a problem.

My instincts were right. When he started building a big, new home, the money stopped flowing back to Indiana. When I found out the money was going into his house instead, I sent our sales manager to Los Alamos, California, where the business was, to fire the man and take over the operation. He did just that and moved the business to Huntington Beach. We kept it there until

2003, when our dealer network became so strong in California that we no longer needed to have a physical presence there.

Our expansion into New Jersey was about going to where the population was. By having a presence there, we could easily access New Jersey, New York City, Connecticut, Pennsylvania, and the Mid-Atlantic states. There's not much of a story to be told with that location, because once our dealer network was able to be self-sufficient, we shut down New Jersey, too.

Going international was a completely different process. We now sell our products in every corner of the world, but I'll briefly talk about just one: Australia.

Our activities in Australia started when a couple, Roger and Judith Sack, who operated a Brisbane-based family-owned company named Tramanco, came to see me in Winamac. Started by Roger as a one-man operation in 1975, Tramanco supplies and installs leading-edge Australian-designed and Australian-manufactured onboard weighing systems to the transport industry. Tramanco also covers a range of vehicle-mounted wheelchair loaders, wheelchair occupant restraint systems, access seating, and vehicle modifications to allow for wheelchair access. Today, Tramanco is the exclusive distributor of our products in Australia, New Zealand, and Southeast Asia.

Although neither Roger nor Judith was in a wheelchair when they came to see me, they were the first people in Australia to realize the importance of providing wheelchair-seated passengers with safe and secure mobility. After several years of marketing a modified commercial tailgate loader as a wheelchair loader, Roger had gone on an extended search for such purpose-built equipment and had ended up at my door.

In the ensuing years, Roger has worked hard to understand our business and has traveled to Winamac each year to supplement his knowledge and learn how to build his own network of dealers.

Along with his wife, Judith, who is also a director of Tramanco, he has become very successful in distributing our products to the Australian marketplace. In keeping with our focus on providing the highest-quality products, Roger is a member of various Standards Australia committees, which are producing standards for the safety of disabled passengers, and is the representative of the Commercial Vehicle Industry Association of Australia on Standards Australia.

Roger has been a big contributor to our success, and his dedication to learning and growth is exactly what we looked for as we grew our dealer network. We needed that dealer network as advances in medicine, returning veterans, and an aging population created more and more people who needed the products we had to offer. We needed people like Roger who were willing to put in the time and effort to understand our business and get close to their customers; I believe much of my success has been in finding those people.

As I've said before, our customers place a certain amount of trust in us and our products. They've suffered serious injuries as the result of accidents, gotten terrible wounds in defense of our country or been born with disabling diseases. As a person who has spent most of his life in a chair, I know what people like me go through. I know the physical and emotional pain they have to deal with as they live their daily lives. Life for them is hard enough as it is. The last thing they need is a product that leaves them stranded when all they want is something they can rely on to be there when they need it.

Although it may sound corny, our customers cannot be let down; they must be lifted up. I've dedicated my life to fulfilling that very proposition.

chapter nineteen

LET'S MAKE A DEALER

Reform business when business is good.
-- Hiroshi Okuda, Former Toyota
Chairman and President

AS A longtime race fan, I've noticed that drivers who consistently win seem to take the same approach: when they're ahead, they floor it. In fact, Mario Andretti, the only driver in history to win the Indianapolis 500, the Daytona 500, and the Formula One World Championship, once said, "If you feel like you're under control, you're just not going fast enough."

Andretti, and those who end up in the winner's circle, believe that being in the lead is no time to admire the scenery and wave to the crowd; it's time to put the pedal to the metal. I feel the same way about business. That's why, after many successful years of primarily selling directly to our customers, we decided to change our go-to-market approach and set up a network of dealers who could champion our products and give us a much wider and more effective distribution.

Like most good things that happen in our business, the creation of our dealer network started with our customers themselves, who came to me and asked whether they could start selling our products. Needing a better method of distribution, I agreed to give it a try. It worked immediately and still does. More often than not, dealers who start out as our customers are the most successful. Why is that?

To begin with, when dealers have been customers first, they don't have to guess what it's like to live life in a wheelchair. That goes for whether they themselves are disabled or they have a friend or family member who is in a wheelchair. As a result, they don't have to imagine what their customers are going through and then try to explain it to them. They know, firsthand, the frustration and inconvenience of not being able to do whatever they feel like doing, when they feel like doing it, and go where they feel like going. They know what it's like to encounter stairs where there should be a ramp or an elevator. They know what it's like to go to a restaurant or any other building where the proper accommodations have not been made. They know what it's like to try to drag themselves in and out of vehicles that are ill suited to transporting them. They know what it's like to sit at home because it's too hard to deal with it all.

At the same time, because many of our dealers started out as customers, they know the freedom our products give them. They know the concerns that visitors to their dealerships have because they have the same concerns. I'm not saying dealers who have not experienced life in a wheelchair aren't good dealers, but throughout our company's history, the fact is that some of our best dealers started out as customers.

The idea of selling motor vehicles through a dealer network was of course not new. Though I've been in business almost 50 years, automobile dealers have been around more than twice that long.

In that time, dealers have undergone tremendous change; in many ways, our evolution has been much like theirs.

To put the extent of the change in perspective, let's look at history. The first gasoline-powered car in America, built by the brothers Frank and Charles Duryea in 1893, had its first road trial on September 21 of that year in Springfield, Massachusetts. It was a crude device—a used horse-drawn buggy with a low-tension ignition, spray carburetor, friction transmission, and four-horse-power, one-cylinder gasoline engine. Apparently, this test-drive was not the success they hoped it would be because they drove it once more, one and a half months later, and then shelved it.

Three years later, Henry Ford sold his first car, a Quadracycle, for $200. He used the proceeds from the sale to build another car and then some prototypes, but he didn't sell another car until 1903.

In 1896, Ransom E. Olds, who was the first mass producer of gasoline-powered automobiles in the United States, built his first model, but he didn't start selling his cars until 1899.

With the Duryea, Ford, and Olds stories as a backdrop, perhaps my first motorized wheelchair, which I test-drove in my mother's kitchen, and my first conversion of a van, which was the lift I installed in the post office Jeep in my parents' garage, weren't that bad after all. The minute I finished both of them, like Henry Ford, I used the money I made to build new and improved ones, and then I repeated the process each time I made a sale.

As for the automakers, although they had gotten off to a slow start, they soon went into overdrive. However, while dozens of manufacturers were making thousands of cars by the year 1900, they still had to figure out how to sell them. As was the case with our wheelchairs and vans, these upstart automakers tried numerous methods of marketing and selling—through factory-owned and factory-operated storerooms, consignment, catalogs, and even traveling salesmen.

At Braun, we tried many of the same routes to market, including driving all over the country with a converted van. Ultimately, we discovered that just as the early auto manufacturers had needed a better distribution system, so did we. Like the car companies, we soon realized the answer was to cultivate a network of independent dealers and businesses. Besides being an efficient and effective way to get our products in the hands of our customers, working with dealers was a good idea for everyone involved.

Our first dealers were customers who opened a dealership in Georgia after buying one of our first converted vans for their son, Buddy. Until they sold the business many years later, they were one of the most successful dealers in our network. Just as my parents had done, Buddy's mother and father were committed to giving him a mainstream life—so much so that they had driven straight to Indiana to get him one of my early conversion vans. As a result, providing mobility became a passion for them. Before long, that passion grew to the point they put their hearts and souls into helping others meet their mobility needs. They worked hard at understanding our business, and I personally spent a lot of time helping them along.

You know, I've had people ask me why I haven't used my knowledge and experience from a lifetime of manufacturing to offer my services as a consultant to other companies. My answer is simple: I did act as a consultant, but I did it with my own network of dealers. I taught them, and they, in turn, taught me. We created the mobility industry together, and with any luck, we'll sustain it together far into the future.

I love working closely with our dealers because, like me, they are risk takers and pioneers. I still talk with many of our dealers every day and ask and answer questions, listen to their concerns, and give guidance where I can. For their part, our dealers make good use of the product and service training we provide at our company headquarters. Each year, they flock to Winamac to see the latest products, hear what's in the pipeline, and become experts on our offerings.

In the beginning of the automotive industry, its development was also driven by risk takers and pioneers. Of course, the Internet did not exist, and, before long, the car dealerships that were housed in storefronts soon expanded into purpose-built car showrooms and repair shops. Because the auto industry was just getting started, carmakers and dealers popped up one day and were gone the next. In order to keep their newborn businesses alive, many of the early dealers carried cars from several different companies so they could spread their risk should some of the automakers fail; therefore, they would be assured of always having vehicles on hand to offer customers. Often, the agreement to become a dealer was simply made with a handshake, an exchange of a small amount of money, and an agreement to accept one or two cars.

With our company, it was much the same. We had no lengthy contracts, no massive commitments of capital, and no heavy-handed agreements that demanded firstborn sons from dealers in order to carry our products. We also relied on handshakes, people keeping their word, and the beliefs that we were on to something and that if everyone worked hard and played fair, we would all be successful.

By 1920, approximately 15,000 automotive dealers and 600 manufacturers were in existence. With many carmakers going out of business after making just a couple of models, banks were wary of lending money to companies in an industry that was still in its infancy. These carmakers may have been inventors, engineers, and mechanics, but many of them lacked the business acumen necessary for banks to bet on them with money. Even automakers that had been in business for a while had a difficult time coming up with the funds they needed to finish their projects and keep the doors open.

Today, a consortium of many large banks handles the financing for our business, but for decades, our company was seen as too great a risk and we couldn't obtain any credit. When we finally did get a credit line, we didn't use it, and we stuck to our pay-as-you-go philosophy, which turned out to be a blessing in disguise. For us, getting a credit line from a bank was really more of a way for us to show we had enough customers and enough demand for the manufacturers to take us seriously. I am not the sort of person to say "I told you so," but I sometimes wonder how the local bank that threw me out when I first asked for a loan would have fared if it would have had faith in my prospects and done business with me.

For the early automakers, independent dealers provided a solution to the problem of raising enough money to keep manufacturing cars. These dealers sent the manufacturers large deposits on new automobiles, which provided the funding for the continued operation of assembling cars. In those early years, selling cars was not difficult. By 1920, consumers bought cars faster than manufacturers could make them. With so much cash flowing into car company coffers from car dealers, carmakers didn't even need to keep accurate books or predict what future sales would be. The orders rolled in, and the cars rolled out.

With our business, a dealer didn't have to pay anything to get an agreement to sell our converted vans and lifts. The case was the same with the early carmakers. If a manufacturer thought a dealer would properly represent its products, it got a dealership. Besides the required couple of pages of legal language, the dealer's agreement included a map and a definition of its sales territory. The agreement stipulated that the dealer did not have exclusive rights to sell in its defined territory and that the manufacturer could still sell from its factory store if it wanted to. The idea was not to take advantage of the dealers but to ensure a steady supply of cars to meet the exploding demand.

The contract also had a stipulation that the dealer would have a building out of which it could make sales and provide service for the products it carried. This might not sound like that big of a deal, but customers needed a place they could come to—with proper signage signifying this was an authorized dealer—so they could "kick the tires" and get their questions answered about this new-fangled product that was not too far removed from being called a "horseless carriage."

Having a physical presence through our dealer network was—and is—a critical component of the relationship we have with our customers. When the Internet came along in the early 1990s, a lot of people talked about how that technology would eliminate the need for the go-between in all industries, including dealers. In the automotive industry, pundits surmised that customers would buy vehicles online and have them shipped to their homes, without ever having to see what they were buying. To them, cars were nothing more than commodities that could be bought and sold online, like pet food, which rather famously also didn't survive existing solely on the Internet.

In reality, something different happened. Because the Internet provided customers with easy accessibility to information, they were flooded with empty claims, both by well-meaning and eager companies and by people trying to make a fast buck. As a result, customers were confused and sought help from knowledgeable experts—like our dealers—who could provide context for all the information they were being bombarded with.

Having a dealer network or a Web presence is not an either/or proposition for us; we must have both. Our products are somewhat more sophisticated than others and will always need some explanation. That is where our dealers can explain, in real time, what the products are all about, how they work, and how they can or can't be altered to meet a person's specific needs. On the other hand, our customers are smart people who have a lot invested—both in expense and in their need for reliability—in choosing products that meet their needs, and for them, the Internet is a vital research tool. For our company, our Web site is another way for us to communicate with both our customers and our dealers. Instead of making our dealers expendable, the Internet enables us to drive traffic to our dealers, which increases their importance that much more.

By 1990, with our dealer network in place, our products firmly established in the minds and lives of our customers, and societal attitudes toward the disabled shifting in our favor, we were ready for hypergrowth, and that's just what we got.

chapter twenty

INVENTING THE FUTURE

I just invent then wait until man comes around
to needing what I've invented.

-- R. Buckminster Fuller, Inventor and architect

THE NECESSITY of finding reliable mobility led me to create an invention and a company that changed my life and the lives of thousands of individuals worldwide. In many ways, my "disability" led to one valuable "ability," knowing firsthand the frustration of having your independence held back because society doesn't think you deserve an invitation to the party.

Today, most of society sees the ability in each individual, disabled or not, and that shift in attitude has been a blessing to our company and the disabled community. I'd like to think our products played a small role in this shift, simply because they allowed people with disabilities to get out in society and start demanding their rights. Today's world is different from the one I faced when I started Save-a-Step Manufacturing as a part-time business in my parents' garage. Since that time, walls have been torn down, ramps have been built in their place, and the Braun Corporation has become a multifaceted company providing mobility to every corner of the globe.

As society began to change, we decided the time had come for a change of our own. In 2007, we started to market our consumer products under the name BraunAbility. The name is an appropriate merging of our solid history of quality products with our focus toward the future and the ability within each of our customers. Our goal is no less than to redefine the ability industry in the years to come, one customer at a time. Our new tagline says it all: "Because life is a moving experience."

But I'm getting a little ahead of myself. Several pieces had to fall into place before we became BraunAbility. I look back on the 1990s and early 2000s as a period of tremendous growth, both for our company and in society's attitude toward individuals with disabilities.

With the passage of the Americans with Disabilities Act of 1990, the disabled community was awarded unprecedented access to public places. In the same time frame, we introduced a revolutionary new product called the Entervan. This lowered-floor minivan offered unparalleled ease of access for wheelchair users, and it quickly became the flagship of our product line as thousands of consumers all over the world discovered a newfound independence. Together, these two events caused our company's growth to skyrocket.

Let me start with the Entervan, a lowered-floor minivan conversion based on the ever popular "soccer mom" vehicles launched in the 1980s. Today, these vans continue to be our most popular products.

Consumers flocked to the Entervan because of its quality, easy-to-use design, and, maybe most important, the fact that it looked just like the vehicles parked in the neighbors' driveway. It blended in with the rest of the vehicles on the road, something a full-sized van with a raised top never did.

To most people, a full-sized van was a truck. It was something small businesses, trade workers, and delivery people used. A minivan was more mainstream and fit in comfortably with the flow of society because it had the characteristics of a passenger car, which people were already driving and were used to; it could fit in a parking garage or parking space with no trouble; and it didn't require people to lift themselves up into the much larger and more inaccessible interior. In addition, with our Entervan, people didn't have to enter via a lift but instead could roll their chairs right up the ramp. In full-sized vans, passengers in wheelchairs had to ride in the midsection or the rear of the van; in a minivan, because the front seats were easily removable, they could go right up front and sit where they wanted to, whether they were a passenger or the driver. The Entervan's dropped floor also enabled a person in a wheelchair to sit at the same level as other passengers and see the same things everyone else was seeing. Most people took this for granted but not wheelchair users. To them, this was revolutionary.

In the early days of using converted full-sized vans, consumers were just happy to be mobile. They were happy they could get in a vehicle and go do whatever they felt like doing. Just leaving their house without having to organize logistics a week in advance gave them newfound liberty, freedom, and independence.

Pardon the pun, but in those days, comfort and style took a backseat to pure access. It didn't matter so much that a person in a wheelchair sat in the back, away from the conversation that was taking place in the front of the vehicle; it didn't matter that they were raised up so high they couldn't see outside; it only mattered that they could get somewhere.

With the Entervan, not only could they get somewhere, but they could get there in comfort and style. While the full-sized van still plays an important part in the transportation of wheelchair users, the minivan has become the number-one choice.

In order to keep up with the success of the Entervan and the revolution that the ADA presented, we made a significant investment in our facilities in Winamac. We'd already added a 100,000-square-foot plant in the late '80s that focused on wheelchair lift production as well as parts fabrication. It soon became obvious we'd need even more manufacturing space to accommodate minivan production. There was just one problem: we'd run out of real estate.

I tried to negotiate for a property just west of Winamac that was recently vacated by Winamac Steel, a division of Detroit Steel, but I didn't care for the price they gave me. Eventually, I did acquire the property—and at quite a deal, I might add. Once again, I found myself in the right place at the right time.

As I mentioned before, I've never been able to take up typical hobbies like golf or skiing; instead, I took on less conventional pastimes. When my family vacationed in Clearwater, Florida, I started buying and selling real estate as a hobby for about 10 or 15 years. At one point, my real estate broker came up with a building that was vacated when the savings and loan banks went under in the late '80s. The empty facility was big—more than 80,000 square feet—and was on a major thoroughfare in Clearwater with over 75,000 vehicles passing by each day.

I didn't know what I'd do with the building, but the price was right for a facility on such a highly traveled roadway. I went ahead with the deal and immediately found a tenant, a company who manufactured ADA-compatible signs that businesses would need in order to comply with the new legislation. We signed a three-year lease agreement with them.

Not long after, I had an idea: what if I traded this Clearwater facility for the building I wanted back home? I called Detroit Steel's broker, and he agreed to come with me down to Florida to check out the property. We took him up on the building's roof and stood there watching the cars stream by on the highway below. After a few minutes, I said, "There are more than 75,000 cars driving by here every day. Which would you rather have: this location or an abandoned building on Highway 14 in Winamac, Indiana?"

He took the Florida building, and I wound up with a new international headquarters for the Braun Corporation.

We didn't buy it or build it; we made an open trade for it, at quite a cost advantage for us. What would have cost $30 a square foot to build we bought for only $3 a square foot—just 10% of what we would have spent on a brand-new facility. We now had an additional 150,000 square feet of manufacturing space to fill up. When we first started to move our equipment and offices into the new space, I know a lot of us had the same thought: "Man, we'll never fill all of this!"

Actually, we wasted no time filling it. We needed space to accommodate sales, engineering, and product support departments, which were all expanding to keep up with the rapid pace. Headquarters wasn't the only thing expanding; our dealer network was also growing by leaps and bounds. To keep our dealers up to speed on the latest product developments, we added classroom and meeting space for hands-on product workshops and service schools held throughout the year. Years later, we added another plant where we manufactured commercial paratransit units. After decades of steady growth, we are now bursting at the seams again today.

Although the Entervan has accounted for a substantial percentage of our growth, it's not the only innovation we introduced in those years. A couple of key acquisitions gave us a diverse product line that truly set us apart as the mobility industry leader. First came the 1996 Mobile Tech acquisition that gave us the under-vehicle lift (UVL). A few years later, we made another important acquisition, this one of Crow River, a lift manufacturer based in Brooten, Minnesota. Crow River offered the Vangater, an electric lift with a unique folding platform that allowed ambulatory access to the side door of full-sized vans. Personal mobility isn't one-size-fits-all, and these two products helped diversify our line of commercial and consumer lifts.

We've made a commitment to customer satisfaction, and whether it's through a survey from our product support department or a conversation I have with a fellow wheelchair user at a Colts game, we take all of our customers' suggestions seriously.

This commitment to customer satisfaction led to a very important decision in 2004. We acquired a company by the name of Independent Mobility Systems (IMS), a competitor headquartered in Farmington, New Mexico, that manufactured its own lowered-floor conversion called the Rampvan. We had heard many, many customers expressing interest in a conversion based on an "import" minivan. By adding the popular Toyota Sienna to our fleet of conversions, we were even better positioned to satisfy the varied tastes of our customers. By doing so, we also became the exclusive mobility converter of Toyota vans. This was an important strategic relationship for us that remains in place to this day.

As I said at the beginning of this chapter, the passage of the Americans with Disabilities Act (ADA)—which celebrates its 20th anniversary in 2010—had an enormous impact on our company. Because of the unprecedented access the law provided for people with disabilities, more people than ever before sought solutions to their mobility needs. They got it through our paratransit vehicles and full-sized vans, but by far the biggest demand was for our Entervan, which came along at just the right time. As a result, newly empowered consumers asking for our Entervan flocked by the thousands to our dealers, who were more than happy to meet their needs.

Those who were unaware of the history of disability rights or the history of our company may have gotten the mistaken impression that the ADA was responsible for our success. In other words, they thought that because the ADA was passed, we formed a company and took advantage of the legislation to become a global sensation. As readers of my story have hopefully learned by now, the opposite is true: it was the decades-long effort of our company and the effort of more than a hundred groups dedicated to disability rights, civil rights, and social justice that joined forces to ensure its passage. It was a great day for everyone, including yours truly.

On the morning of July 26, 1990, with approximately 3,000 disability rights advocates, members of Congress, and President George H. W. Bush's administration looking on, the president signed the ADA into law. It was the largest presidential signing ceremony in history, and my very good friend Beverly Chapman, who since passed away in 1993, was on hand to witness it.

In his remarks on the south lawn of the White House that day, President Bush described the ADA as "the world's first comprehensive declaration of the equality of people with disabilities and evidence of America's leadership internationally in the cause of human rights. With today's signing of the landmark Americans with Disabilities Act, every man, woman, and child with a disability can now pass through once-closed doors, into a bright new era of equality, independence, and freedom … Let the shameful wall of exclusion finally come tumbling down."

The president traced the ADA's roots in American history back through the Civil Rights Act of 1964 to the Declaration of Independence, saying: "We are keeping faith with the spirit of our ... forefathers who wrote ... 'We hold these truths to be self-evident that all men are created equal, that they are endowed by their Creator with certain inalienable rights.' This act is powerful in its simplicity. It will ensure that people with disabilities are given the basic guarantees for which they have worked so long and so hard—independence, freedom of choice, control of their lives, the opportunity to blend fully and equally into the rich mosaic of the American mainstream."

That special word, "mainstream," brings us full circle. It's what my mother and father demanded for me on that hot summer day in 1946 when I was given my death sentence. It's what I demanded for myself as I strove to find my way in the world and follow their bright, shining example. It's what I demanded for others who faced the same challenges I had and who desired more than anything in life to rise above those challenges.

In closing, let me say this: as I continue to climb the ladder of life, I hope with all my heart that I never have to have you or your loved ones as customers. But if you should need us, we will be here, ready and willing to extend a helping hand.

Rise above, my friends, and reach back to help others climb the ladder of life.

I am only one, but I am one. I cannot do
everything, but I can do something.
And I will not let what I cannot do interfere
with what I can do.

-- Edward Everett Hale

I'M GOING to ask you to take one more trip with me.

Imagine it's 1946 and you're my parents, Joseph and Olive Braun. A doctor at Riley Hospital in Indianapolis has just told you that your six-year-old son has muscular dystrophy. He says your boy won't make it through his teen years. You stare in horror. Choke back tears. Get light-headed and shuffle your feet.

The doctor looks at you with pity. He suggests you leave your son behind so he can be examined further, not just for a few days but for weeks. He says sure, your son will be able to walk for a few years, but gradually he'll get weaker, until one day, he won't be able to walk at all. He won't be able to feed himself, go to the bathroom alone, or bathe in solitude. He'll lie in bed or, at best, sit in a chair, until his suffering is over.

He says you have a choice. You can walk out the door with your son. You can take him back to Winamac and put a tremendous strain on yourselves, on the daughter you already have, and, most of all, on the boy himself.

Or, he says, you can walk out the door alone. You can let him live in peace, in a place where he can be cared for properly—and studied. In this very hospital, thanks to your boy, scientific discoveries might be made that will save the lives of others or at least make their lives more manageable.

Of course, by now you know the decision my parents made. For them, there really was no agonizing doorway dilemma. They were going to leave, and they were going to take me with them. Once in the car, I'd take my familiar place in the back seat and would make faces at my sister, just like I did on the way down there.

I must tell you that the possibility for the other choice was there. If it weren't for Joseph and Olive Braun, another choice may very well have been made.

Now I ask you to imagine that you're me, today, at the age of 69. As a CEO of a global company, a father of five supportive children, a grandfather of eight, a husband to a wonderful wife, and the son of Joseph Braun, who passed away on February 7, 1986, and the ever-stalwart 98-year-old Olive Braun of Winamać, Indiana, I am still climbing the ladder of life.

This year, I was faced with my own doorway decision. I am painfully aware that some people in the world do not have full use of their arms or legs; they have been in a car accident, have become paralyzed on the job, or have been injured in combat while serving our country. People have multiple sclerosis, cerebral palsy, or spinal muscular atrophy, like I do. These are people who may never complain but who are nonetheless quietly desperate because they never leave their homes. People of all shapes and sizes, through no fault of their own, cannot do the things they would like to do.

What does that have to do with me, you ask? I know the world is full of people who could use wheelchair vans but who cannot afford them. I know this because I am inundated with requests from people who are dealing with the same mobility challenges I am but do not have the financial means to overcome those challenges.

Faced with that knowledge of need, how could I go out the door alone and leave these good people behind? To use my father's example, after he reached back with his hand to help me up the ladder of life, how could I not help others? Granted, I can't help everyone, but I've always been struck by the words of the minister Edward Everett Hale, who said, "I am only one, but I am one. I cannot do everything, but I can do something. And I will not let what I cannot do interfere with what I can do."

How could I sit by idly while others called out in obvious need? I'd already overcome the challenge of mobility by inventing the motorized scooter and wheelchair lift. I'd already found my way past the obstacles erected by society's schools, restaurants, and banks. I'd already been helped by people like my mom and dad, my children, Ralph Rocky, Paul Gillette, Beverly Chapman, Becky Kroft, my wife Melody, and countless other angels.

If I'd already risen above the challenge of mobility and made a living helping those who could afford my products do the same, how could I not help others who were not so fortunate?

Faced with these choices, my decision was easy: I would do whatever I could to help those in need. That was the driving force behind the creation of the Ralph Braun Foundation this year, whose mission will be to help provide accessible transportation to those without the financial resources to purchase BraunAbility products.

Once again, I know the need is great.

For instance, Medicaid and Medicare typically cover the purchase price of power wheelchairs. However, they draw the line there and do not offer any assistance for vehicle transportation. Ironically, this means that Medicaid and Medicare offer people mobility by funding power wheelchairs, but they don't allow them to go anywhere with them.

In reality, while mobility is essential to a person's social and mental health, the wheelchair itself is only the first piece of the puzzle. A power chair offers access only to the home and maybe the surrounding blocks in the neighborhood. A BraunAbility wheelchair van completes the mobility puzzle and picks up where others leave off.

Moreover, while I've always gotten letters from people who would love to have wheelchair vans, the number increased exponentially when we ran a contest last year called "The Ultimate Fan Van Giveaway," in which Toyota, Great Clips, and Braun Racing teamed up with BraunAbility to give away a one-of-a-kind Toyota Sienna wheelchair van styled like a race car.

We've already established that I love racing, love cars, and love banging metal together, so in my mind, the Ultimate Fan Van is a mobile piece of art. It's an amazingly accurate replica of Braun Racing's #38 car, which races in the NASCAR Nationwide Series. From its red and white suede seats to the custom vinyl graphics, this wheelchair van is one tricked-out ride.

To enter the contest, entrants wrote an essay answering the question "How will the Ultimate Fan Van make a difference in my life?" To give you an idea of the need and of the quality of the entries, take a look at the following:

"Can someone please help me? I am at my wits' end. I have a 16-year-old son who has spastic quadriplegia cerebral palsy and is confined to a wheelchair. Day by day as

he grows, my husband and I are less able to take him out into the community because we do not have a van. Often he spends Friday afternoon until Monday in the house until he can be picked up by his school bus and go back out 'into the world.' I have tried to get financed for a van to no avail and was just forced to take a 10 percent pay cut in this unstable economy. My son is a bright, creative, and expressive child, but I can already see that I have stifled his independence and abilities by not being able to provide him the necessary means of transportation."

This is only one example, with thousands more just like it. We heard from many, many individuals who have the need for reliable mobility but not the means to obtain it. I hope BraunAbility and the Ralph Braun Foundation, working together, will help meet this need far into the future.

I have a very clear vision of this future, where people faced with unimaginable obstacles pull together to overcome them. That includes you, the reader of this book, who, no matter what you're dealing with, holds the future in your very own hands.

After all, if I can rise above, so can you.

acknowledgments

I'M GRATEFUL to many individuals for their help and encouragement while writing this book, from concept to completion. To avoid leaving anyone behind, I'll just say thank you to everyone who offered advice and assistance throughout this rewarding project.

Of course, I have many more people to thank for growing The Braun Corporation into a successful company. To my family, employees, and close friends, thank you for your dedication. I've always said my greatest strength is the ability to surround myself with good people. Thanks for joining me on this ride.

RALPH W. BRAUN was founder and CEO of BraunAbility, the largest manufacturer of wheelchair lifts and wheelchair-accessible vehicles in the world. He was an innovator and pioneer of the mobility industry and passed away in February, 2013 at the age of 72.

For more information about the Ralph Braun Foundation,
please visit
www.ralphbraunfoundation.org

To learn about BraunAbility minivans and wheelchair lifts,
or to find the BraunAbility dealer nearest you,
please visit
www.braunability.com